JOURNAL *of* MUSEUM EDUCATION

VOLUME 34 ❧ NUMBER 3 ❧ FALL 2009
A PUBLICATION OF THE MUSEUM EDUCATION ROUNDTABLE

Building Diversity in Museums

ISBN 978-1-59874-822-2

Journal of Museum Education (ISSN: 1059-8650), is published three times yearly, in the Spring, Summer, and Fall, by Left Coast Press, Inc., in partnership with the Museum Education Roundtable. The journal publishes original papers on theory, training, and practice in the museum education field. Each issue focuses on a specific theme of interest to professional and informal museum educators, administrators, and practitioners.

Subscriptions: All subscription inquiries should be sent to Left Coast Press, Inc., at the address below, addressed to the attention of the Journal Manager. Institutional subscriptions may be purchased via check, VISA, MasterCard, or purchase order. All non-institutional subscriptions should be prepaid by personal check, VISA, or MasterCard. Make checks payable to Left Coast Press, Inc. Current prices are listed on the publisher's website, or may be obtained by contacting the publisher at the address below. Payment in U.S. dollars only.

International Orders and Shipping: Add $15.00 per year for postage outside the United States.

Claims: Claims for missing copies will be honored for up to 12 months after date of publication. Missing copies due to losses in transit can be replaced pending availability of reserve stock.

Change of Address: Please notify the publisher six weeks in advance of address changes. Send old address label along with new address to ensure proper identification, and specify name of journal. *Postmaster:* Send all change of address to Left Coast Press, Inc., *Journal of Museum Education*, 1630 N. Main Street, #400, Walnut Creek, CA 94596.

Advertising: Current rates and specifications can be obtained by contacting the Journals Manager, Left Coast Press, Inc., at the address below.

Back issues: Back issues are available through Left Coast Press, Inc., at the address below.

Copyright Permission: For reprint permission requests please contact the publisher, Left Coast Press, Inc., at the address below.

Submission Guidelines: *The Journal of Museum Education* (JME) welcomes the submission of original proposals for issues on theory, training, and practice in the museum education field. Topics are proposed by guest editors who develop a theme, recruit authors, and coordinate communication between authors and the Editor-in-chief. Proposals and all manuscripts are subject to peer review by knowledgeable scholars and professional practitioners and, if accepted, may be subject to revision. Materials submitted to *JME* should not be under consideration by other publishers, nor should they be previously published in any form. Electronic submissions of issue proposals should include a cover letter, issue abstract, proposed articles and/or authors, and the guest editor's resume. *JME* does not accept unsolicited, single articles for publication. For details on upcoming issue themes, manuscript composition, size, formatting, etc., please consult the Left Coast Press web site (www.lcoastpress.com) or Museum Education Roundtable web site (www.museumeducation.info). Reference style should conform to the Chicago Manual of Style, 15th edition. Non-conforming manuscripts will be returned to the author(s) for revision.

Send issue proposals and manuscript correspondence to Tina Nolan, Interim Editor, *Journal of Museum Education*, via email: *JMuseEd@gmail.com*.

Production and Composition by Detta Penna, Penna Design

Printed in the United States of America

Left Coast Press, Inc.
1630 N. Main Street, #400
Walnut Creek, CA 94596
Phone (925) 935-3380, Fax (925) 935-2916
email journals@lcoastpress.com, web www.lcoastpress.com

JOURNAL *of* MUSEUM EDUCATION

A PUBLICATION OF THE MUSEUM EDUCATION ROUNDTABLE

Interim Editor
TINA R. NOLAN
Associate Director of Partnerships, National College of Education,
National-Louis University

Building Diversity in Museums

Guest Editors
SYRUS MARCUS WARE
Program Coordinator, Art Gallery of Ontario

GILLIAN MCINTYRE
Program Coordinator, Art Gallery of Ontario

Editorial Advisors

AMELIA CHAPMAN, Curator of Education, Pacific Asia Museum

CYNTHIA COPELAND, Principal, The OutSourced Muse

MARIA DEL CARMEN COSSU, International Arts and Early Childhood Education,
Smithsonian Early Enrichment Center

MARK HOWELL, Director of Education, American Civil War Center at Historic Tredegar

LYNN MCRAINEY, Director of Education, Chicago History Museum

LAURA ROBERTS, Director of the Boston Center for Adult Education and
principal at Roberts Consultant, Strategic Thinking for Cultural Nonprofits

SUSAN SPERO, Associate Professor, Museum Studies, John F. Kennedy University

The Museum Education Roundtable (MER) is a nonprofit organization based in Washington, DC, dedicated to enriching and promoting the field of Museum Education. Through publications, programs, and communication networks, MER fosters professionalism, encourages leadership, scholarship, and research in museum-based learning, and advocates the inclusion and application of museum-based learning in the general education arena.

For more information on MER and its activities, please contact on the web at www.museumeducation.info. Members receive the Journal of Museum Education as a benefit of membership. Write to MER at PO Box 15727, Washington, DC 20003.

Building Diversity in Museums

Gillian McIntyre & Syrus Marcus Ware

"…identities are the names we give to the different ways we are positioned by, and position ourselves within the narratives of the past."
> *Stuart Hall, "Cultural Identity and Diaspora," In Williams, Patrick & Laura Chrisman eds.,* Colonial Discourse & Postcolonial Theory: A Reader. *Harvester Wheatsheaf, 1993.*

We work in the Education Department of the Art Gallery of Ontario (AGO), located in the diverse and multicultural city of Toronto. The AGO is a large institution, with a collection of mainly "Western" art. The Gallery recently underwent a Frank Gehry designed reconstruction. While under construction AGO staff strategized to transform the institutional vision alongside the physical changes to become truly relevant in the 21st century. To this end all initiatives across the institution - from exhibition planning to gallery acquisitions to public programming - follow the guiding principles of diversity, relevance, responsiveness, creativity, form and transparency. The new overarching mandate of the AGO is that the visitor experience is paramount. We wish to experiment with new ways of working to engage the broadest audiences possible, realizing that this will necessitate systemic change.

We define diversity broadly, including but not limited to: ability; age; culture; education; economic status; ethnicity; gender identity; immigration status; religion; sexual orientation etc. Although a great deal has been written about diversity in the museum context, the work generated on the subject is not yet significantly reflected in practice. To quote Mark O'Neill, Head of Museums and Galleries, Glasgow City Council: "Relevance, accessibility and inclusiveness are 'vacuous slogans'." (*The People Versus* in Engage review issue 11, Summer 2002. editor Karen Raney)

The language around diversity is shifting and often contested. Terms like 'social inclusion' and 'community cohesion' are currently favoured over 'diversity' and 'new internationalism' is steadily replacing 'multiculturalism'. Language is an interesting indicator of evolving and complex cultural shifts. It is at best a guide for communication and understanding, and at worst something that limits our thoughts and encourages stereotyping. It is informative to reflect on the effect of language on our thoughts. For example, what do we think when we hear the words: senior, minority, 'at risk' youth, ethnic, disabled, elderly etc.? What labels would we choose to describe ourselves? What are the challenges in creating open and flexible, evolving museums for the vast range of individuals in the communities and societies they serve?

In 2008 the AGO initiated a 15 member cross-departmental Diversity Advisory Group. Its mandate is described as follows:

> To advocate for an inclusive AGO and advise Leadership Team of opportunities for, and obstacles to, the AGO's commitment to diversity in its visitor base, and, ultimately, its staff and volunteer ranks. As a resource to the AGO the advisory provides research on best practices in the public art museum sector to inform training, policies and programming toward greater inclusiveness. It also monitors applicable federal and provincial policy and legislation.

So far we have conducted an internal institutional scan of current programs and services and held numerous community consultations. Currently the advisory is focusing on implementing the Accessibility for Ontarians with Disabilities Act which has a goal of making Ontario fully accessible by 2025. As founding members of the Diverstiy Advisory Team, we both have a keen interest in substantial and measurable systemic change.

In this issue there are essays from Britain, Canada and the United States with a balance of theoretical and pragmatic work on a range of topics including such issues as: rethinking notions of diversity in the 21st century; inclusion and diversity in collections and programming; accessibility/disability in museums; LGTBQ issues; and web accessibility.

Jessica Harrington at the Institute of International Visual Arts (Iniva) in London challenges us to consider 'the diversity of diversity now'. Iniva is an institution where the very founding rationale, in 1994, was to help diversify mainstream institutions and challenge the monocultural conception of

British art and culture. Harrington discusses the important issues to consider as Iniva strives to remain engaged and relevant in a changing cultural and artistic environment. We hope that large museums can learn from smaller, and possibly more nimble institutions like Iniva and reposition themselves as sites for social engagement rather than elitist repositories of culture.

Gerald McMaster at the AGO in Toronto talks about the curatorial challenge of reinstalling the Canadian galleries previously hung as a linear art historical progression from 18th century colonial times. Using the AGO's guiding principles these galleries now honour 11,000 years of culture on this land and include First Nations' and women's art previously missing from the story. To explore the potential of engaging broad audiences, and allowing for the past to be reviewed through the lens of the present, the art is linked through the universal issues of power, myth and memory.

Eithne Nightingale at the Victoria and Albert Museum (V&A) in London describes an ambitious cross departmental three year initiative focusing on cultural diversity with an overarching aim to contribute to change in the V&A's policies and procedures. This three strand program involved researching, developing and mining the collections for hidden histories in relation to culturally diverse communities; programming to attract diverse audiences and encourage interfaith and intercultural understanding and developing partnerships and training aimed at institutional capacity building. Her concluding statement is: "What is self evident is that we are on a journey where diversity becomes central to all that we do".

Stephen Brown, Director of Knowledge Media Design at Du Montfort University, Leicester England, discusses the importance of museums making their contents and services widely available, relevant and useable through Web delivery. Accessibility for Brown refers to the ease with which a wide range of users, including those with disabilities, can use museum Web sites. Brown encourages us to go beyond Internet access and instead focus on issues of usability. He offers theoretical and practical suggestions including a set of simplified accessibility guidelines.

Nancy Arms Simon in San Francisco talks about the project she is working on as she explores the role museums play with individuals of Lesbian, Gay, Transsexual, Bisexual, Queer or Questioning (LGBTQQ) and mixed cultural heritage. Simon suggests strategies for museums targeting these specific individuals as either potential staff or audience members.

Elizabeth Sweeney explores the creation and implementation of accessibility programming at the National Gallery of Canada in Ottawa. Sweeney illustrates how to work with communities to develop relevant programming, and how to work with museums and galleries to adapt programming in a way that meets both public and conservation interests alike. Sweeney highlights the benefits of engaging artists who have created work that is accessible from the outset. Her essay is grounded in disability theory and contemporary art practice.

Tara Turner offers a useful list of diversity resources for further reading on this vast and vital subject.

So where are we going and what will it look like when we get there? Who is currently excluded from our museums and what will it take to make our institutions more democratic? Will greater accessibility lead to a 'dumbing down' (a detestable expression) of scholarship or will standards go up with the resulting plurality of voices and challenges to notions of so-called expertise? How will we achieve systemic change and ensure that diversity issues—or whatever they are called when this happens- are automatically considered at the outset of any planning? One thing is for certain, if we get it right the audiences will follow.

Gillian McIntyre *has a B.A. in Art and Art History ('94) and an M.A. in Museum Studies ('96) from the University of Toronto. Her Masters' thesis explored the relationship between the Art Gallery of Ontario (AGO) and so-called minority communities. McIntyre's responsibilities as Adult Program Coordinator at the AGO have included interpretive planning and community consultation for a new African gallery, installed in 2008. McIntyre also designs and coordinates the AGO's adult public programs. She is a founding member of the AGO's Diversity Advisory Group.*

In 1997 McIntyre initiated Teens Behind the Scenes, a youth volunteer program at the AGO. Between 1998 and 2001 she served as Executive Director of Oakville Arts Council. Amongst other projects during this time she designed and coordinated Telling a Different Story, a three-year on-line anti-racism project. At the same time McIntyre served as President of Community Arts Ontario, an arts service organization. During her tenure she chaired a community arts conference Kicking it up a Notch: Animating Communities in Toronto in 2002. In 2003 she initiated the Cultural Mapping Project. The objective of this project was to diversify the membership and programming of Community Arts Ontario. Between 1991 and 1995 she Chaired Oakville Galleries Board of Directors and is currently a member of the Acquisition Committee.

Syrus Marcus Ware *is a researcher, visual artist and educator. He is the Program Coordinator of the Teens Behind the Scenes program in the education department at the Art Gallery of Ontario. At the AGO, Syrus creates programs for youth under 24 that aim to connect relevant social issues with artistic practice and expression. Syrus has a Hon. B.A in Art History and Visual Studies(2001) and an M.A from the University of Toronto (2010). His Masters thesis explored the experiences of Transsexual/Transgender students at U of T and the diversification of gender within educational settings.*

Syrus has worked several years in the fields of education and advocacy, HIV/AIDS prevention and community education. He is the author of the study "Assessing the HIV/AIDS Service Needs of Trans Communities in Toronto", published by the AIDS Committee of Toronto in 2004. He is a founding member of the Gay, Bi, Queer Trans Men's HIV Prevention Working Group at the Ontario AIDS Bureau, which produced the groundbreaking resource "Primed: The Back Pocket Guide for Trans Guys and the Guys Who Dig 'Em" in 2007. He co-created the Trans-Fathers 2B course at The 519 Community Centre, the first course in North America for Trans guys considering parenting, which first ran in 2007.

Syrus is a program committee member for Mayworks Festival in Toronto and is a past board member of the FUSE magazine. Since 2004, Syrus has been the visual art programmer for the Blockorama Stage, part of Pride Toronto.

Thinking Through Diversity

Jessica Harrington

Abstract   This article considers the history of cultural diversity policy in the UK's visual arts through the questions and research of an art's organisation called Iniva (Institute of International Visual Arts).

In January 2010, Iniva (Institute of International Visual Arts) will present a multi-authored, installation called "Progress Reports: Art in an Era of Diversity" at Rivington Place. Gathering a timeline of archival material, significant events (re-played and new), personal recollections, anecdotes, talks and polemics, this "live documentary" will act as a series of reports into the representation and interpretation of "diversity" in Britain's visual arts over the past fifteen years. Removing diversity from the bureaucratic realm of funding requirements and performance targets where the influence of the imperative often narrows our understanding from exploring the play within diversity, "Progress Reports" will give shape to diversity by exploring the contexts to which it responds and the situations where it finds articulation. Writers, curators, cultural producers and audiences will be invited to collaborate and contribute, to document and debate the role and representation of diversity; to consider what diversity is and what it activates within Britain's contemporary visual arts today.

"Progress Reports" is not a typical Iniva project. It would be hard to say what a typical Iniva project might be, but it follows a typical Iniva format, one of research, debate and discussion, and one of placing a plurality of voices at the heart of its activity. This project arose from an internal discussion, taking place within Iniva over the past few months about its role in the contemporary visual arts today. Last year Stuart Hall (cultural theorist and Iniva's founding Chairman) presented something of a provocative paper to both Iniva staff and board members. Titled "The Changing Landscape of Cultural Diversity in the Visual Arts," the paper was short, only a page in length, but it outlined some

Journal of Museum Education, Volume 34, Number 3, Fall 2009, pp. 203–214.

pressing issues and important questions for the organisation to consider in relation to its direction and vision for the future.

After briefly covering the founding rationale for Iniva's emergence and purpose as driven by a particular objective— *"to help diversify the mainstream institutions, give visibility and critical attention to and support the work of artists coming from and expressing in their work their different cultural backgrounds and the different routes by which they emerged, and to challenge the "monocultural" conception of British art and culture"*— Hall went on to illustrate what he perceived to be significant changes in the landscape of cultural diversity in the visual arts through a succinct list of contextual shifts.

> *The rapid and extensive internationalisation of "the art world," in step with the rapid globalisation of the world— The rise of biennales and international art fairs.*

> *The changes in nature and presence of the "black" minorities in mainstream British society.*

> *The expanded and changing definition of "diversity," given the rapid expansion of new groups and peoples coming as migrants to settle in this country (UK).*

> *The growing unpopularity in public discourse of terms like "multicultural" and "cultural diversity" post 9/11 and 7/7 and the rise of a new goal— "social cohesion."*

Hasn't the requirement of "access" opened the mainstream institutions to the work produced from everywhere— including what used to be the margins? Aren't the different cultures now too "diverse" to be represented?" "Where does the shifting landscape leave Iniva?"[1]

In summary, the paper opened a question on the relevance and vision of an organisation such as Iniva today. While a statement such as this may seem shocking and perhaps hyperbolic, "The Changing Landscape of Cultural Diversity in the Visual Arts" has presented an important and necessary challenge to Iniva's mission and purpose to ensure that Iniva's activities continue to produce meaningful work within its field. By encouraging a "repositioning," a check or audit of current institutional and societal interpretations of "cultural diversity" in comparison, to say, five or ten years ago, Iniva has taken up the challenge to reassess its own engagement with the term by assessing the changing artistic environment around it.

POSITIONING INIVA—THE CONTEXT OF ITS BEGINNINGS.

In 1994, the time of Iniva's inception, the idea, nature, and product of the British art institution was moving through a number of significant changes.

Departing from the perceptions of the museum as repositories of national collections and as "elitist spaces" reserved for those initiated within the disciplines of culture, the museum and the gallery space was increasingly emerging as a space of social engagement. Within the arts, participatory practice was becoming more commonplace and the legacy of institutional critique having had some impact on the public expectation and the reading of the institution, the wider perception of the value of the arts and culture industry was changing.

At the same time, the Arts Council,[2] was in the process of shifting their focus and approach, reflecting the changing cultural scene; moving from their previous role as a provider to and funder of the arts, to a role emphasising the need to widen participation in the arts and to widen audiences while continuing to support development in the field. This acknowledgment of the discussions around accessibility and diversity in the arts (including access to employment, representation in the major national collections, diversity of practitoners, increasing interpretation and education to provide in-roads to interpreting artworks, etc.) has revealed itself through many different responsive strategies.

Another illustration of the drive towards a more inclusive arts scene was a report called "Towards Cultural Diversity: A Report into the Ethnic Minority Arts Action Plan."[3] This report (written in 1989), acted as both a document of the outcomes of the previous three years' "plan" as well as a marker of the council's change in approach. Written by artist Gavin Jantjes, the paper signifies a move away from a debatably separatist perception that saw "ethnic minority arts" almost as a separate cultural scene, being funded by a separate provision, with specific "black cultural centres" being established for "ethnic minority" artists and practitioners[4] to a more inclusive aim "towards cultural diversity." The paper asks us to imagine what the British national culture would look like in the year 2000. It is through this imagining that the concept of cultural diversity is expressed:

> the concept of a broad heterogenous national culture, its make-up reflecting the diversity of cultural achievement issuing from contemporary society. These achievements are not assimilated, but rather placed alongside all other achievements to construct through their diverse autonomies a new superstructure for cultural practice.'[5]

The paper argued for continuing change to be made in the cultural sector, not only in supporting artists and the surrounding cultural field (curators, programming, organizations, and general employment), but in the terminology and conditions through which that support is provided. It highlighted the problematic titling of the "Ethnic Minority Arts Action Plan" and in some ways acted as a call for an understanding of the right for an artist to self-identify, an understanding that to expect an artist to represent or discuss specific issues because of their cultural background or ethnicity (and for that matter gender, sexuality, or disability) was limiting an artistic freedom that would be assumed by other artists. It also signalled the dissolution of "The Ethnic Minority Arts Unit" within the Arts Council and the shift to an "Access Unit" and a "Cultural Diversity Unit."

While this may seem to be a drive led by the Arts Council, the Arts Council were in fact led, influenced, and perhaps provoked by the work of self-organized collectives such as the Pan-Afrikan Connection later known as the blk art group,[6] the Sankofa Collective, and the Black Audio Film Collective,[7] and artists such as Rasheed Araeen, Sunil Gupta, Lubaina Himid, Chila Burman, Gavin Jantjes, Ingrid Pollard, and countless others. The self-organised visibility of these artists and their political stance and drive made them into useful and informative consultants advisors to build the Arts Council's policy.

While these institutional changes were occurring, questions about the parameters of the "British national collection" were voiced with increasing regularity, questions that had been gaining urgency since the seventies; "who" did the "national" collection include and who should it represent? "Who" formed its audiences? Beyond this, "who" and what constituted "British national culture," particularly after the process of decolonization after the Second World War and with the shifting diversity of cultures living in Britain? While these questions might at one point have represented a fear or mourning of the loss of a national identity, the 1990s seemed to embrace this shift towards cultural diversity with "multi-cultural Britain" being high on the political agenda.

The questions posed of the "national" collection opened up inquiries into the dynamic between the national and the international, about the changes in geopolitical contexts, decolonization, and the drive of nation building after the Second World War. The rising frequency of the term "global" as a description of the environment of operation and its consequent effects on our understanding of the "international" were gradually shifting the territorythat the arts scene inhabited. While the International had previously been a term to describe Europe and North America's arts scene, the post-colonial increase in nations lead to a necessary widening of the understanding of the "international."

Beyond the context of the art scene, the world was changing; 1994 saw the World Trade Organization formed, the introduction of "free trade" agreements, change economies, and labor migrate in search of cheaper workers as outsourcing increased. The first user-friendly Internet browser was launched in the spring of '94, and the realm of possibilities for global communication and the consequent effects on finance markets, retail industries and media dissemination began to shift dramatically. Technology enabled a democratization of different practices, and voices were provided the tools with which to make themselves heard. The change in the communications industry had also seen the growth of "Americanization" and the dominant export of "America" as a cultural product. This change, alongside the rapid onset of globalization, raised fears of global homogenization provoking and reasserting resistant trends toward cultural diversity.

Five years after the destruction of the Berlin Wall and all that it had come to symbolize, power dynamics in the world began to change considerably. Previous ideological binaries between communism and capitalism made way for a new ideological binary—that of democracy and fundamentalism. Parts of Europe joined to bolster their negotiating power within the world economy as the European Union under the motto "United in Diversity." The free flow of people, trade, services, and goods in EU countries was a necessary component of the newly formed EU and, as a result, migratory demographics began to change.

It is against this rapidly changing institutional, national, international, and global context that the demand for a new type of arts organization in Britain opened up and why "the emerging concept" of new Internationalism (see Figure 1., New Internationalism—An emerging concept) came to be relevant to investigating the wider international visual arts scene.

INIVA: A PARADIGM FOR A NEW INTERNATIONALIST ARTS ORGANIZATION

The demand to create a new type of visual arts organization which would reflect a different world order to that traditionally promoted and received in Britain through our museums and galleries has often been expressed. (…) there is (…) a greater demand for a space which recognizes a new reality, based on a multiplicity of cultures and an interaction between these which creates a dynamic, pluralistic cultural aesthetic. It is this "new internationalist" aesthetic that will be promoted by Iniva, drawing upon contemporary artistic practice internationally and giving exhibition space to British-based artists.[8]

Iniva began its activities as the Institute of New International Visual Arts, a unique agency with four (later to become five) strands of activity — education and training, publications, research, and exhibitions. The conscious design of it as an organization[9] has allowed it the luxury of determining its precise strategy, shape and structure, ensuring that effective research and consultation can provide it with a robust approach to develop its original vision — to lay the foundation for a greater understanding of the world's contemporary visual arts through developing research and widening understanding of cross cultural and intercultural relations in the visual arts.

While the creation of Iniva was, to some extent, a direct response to the Arts Council's publication on cultural diversity and an opportunity to put this policy into practice, it also existed as an entirely independent project and a response to the swiftly shifting world context in which it was to be situated. "New Internationalism" was a particular reading of this context and a particular expression of cultural diversity in practice, a specific reading that would be furthered by "translating its original concept into tangible programming." The aims of new Internationalism were to reflect the changing picture of the "international" in Britain, documenting its evolving image through the emerging body of both national and international and contemporary artists.

Iniva's quadripartite structure was to ensure that the "new Internationalist aesthetic" and approach could activate change within the different layers of the arts and educational systems in Britain through creating dynamic programming with criticality at its core. Research was a central project of Iniva's structure, commissioning and presenting new research was vital to develop the field, a field that already had an acclaimed following. It forms the heart of Iniva's work, providing material for publications, education and exhibitions, the resource and fuel of Iniva's programming and the routes through to its networks.

Annotating Art's Histories and Global Visions: Towards a New Internationalism in the Visual Arts are both examples of research enacting Iniva's vision through its practice. Both projects began as symposiums, active and collaborative projects to create a live body of work that aim to change the parameters and understanding of art history through their thinking. Annotating Art's Histories performs exactly as the series title claims, pluralizing the discourse of art history through a four-volume publishing project contemplating cultural difference and cross-cultural interaction as dynamic features of twentieth-century art. Each of the volumes provides vital annotations to the traditional, Eurocentric writings of art history, exploring the social, political, and cultural interactions that generate different knowledges and experiences in art's histories. Global Visions was Iniva's first symposium inviting arts practitioners from all over the world to present papers on the subject of new Internationalism, mapping out the terrain of its inquiries and raising questions about the context of its investigations through papers such as "The Non-Sovereign Self," by Gordon Bennett, "The Silent Message of the Museum," by Fred Wilson and "A New Inter–Nationalism: The Missing Hyphen," by Geeta Kapur.

This research formed the "institute" of Iniva's work, not only showing the best of new international practice, but reviewing twentieth-century art history from a new Internationalist perspective. This perspective arose not only as a reworking of traditional Eurocentric ideas of art history, but also through developing and promoting a wider theoretical framework—that of the sociological, political, and cultural factors that affect and provide the context of artistic production.

THE CHANGING LANDSCAPE OF CULTURAL DIVERSITY

Over several sessions, we met as an organization to research and think through different aspects of the questions that Hall had presented to us and what Iniva's response might be — in short, where did the changing landscape of cultural diversity leave Iniva?

The wealth of International bienniales and the building of galleries such as Tate Modern have presented significant changes to the visual arts scene in the UK. It might also be said that there is a wider variety of international artists being shown here as well as larger audiences for the visual arts, particularly the contemporary visual arts. However our understanding and reading of the "International" is still woefully inadequate. Despite the number of global shifts, the changing context of the visual arts in Britain and ever-increasing numbers of International Art Fairs, the meaning that seems to be interpreted from the mainstream "international art" institutions in Britain is that the "International" remains, for the most part, a space of interaction between North America and Europe, often as a result of artists moving to the influential "centres" in order to develop their careers. Art History remains a story narrated in and by particular areas of the world, often told without the contributing details of the contexts and politics of its development. Despite occupying a regular space in the headlines of the British press, the impact of immigration, global movement, and shifting ideologies is barely perceivable through the exhibition content of the mainstream institutions in Britain. Rarely are the geographical movements, geopolitical modifications, and transfers of ideas recognized as contributing factors to the building of an art historical knowledge, even though these factors, among others, could only expand and invigorate our understanding of what an International art history might look like.

So despite the "Internationalization" of the art world—or what might be viewed as the widening of the space of reception for international art—the project of "new Internationalism," as it was once termed, is ongoing. The processes of globalization continue, ensuring that while the ever-shifting geopolitical contexts for art raise new questions, ideas and histories, Iniva will continue to offer a platform where these questions might emerge. Iniva characterises itself as a thinking organisation—one that asks its audiences to "question assumptions about contemporary art and ideas, acting as a catalyst for making those questions part of mainstream culture." So while its focus on new Internationalism may have shifted slightly as the mainstream organizations begin to share an interest in the International visual arts scene, Iniva's role as a "critical friend" continues. This role explores not only the current perceptions of the international within mainstream culture but also the role and changing perceptions of the diversity within Britain's visual arts.

At the time of "Towards Cultural Diversity" going to print in 1989, the political environment was one that aimed (not to say that this was achieved) to celebrate the opportunities that "multi-cultural Britain" had to offer. The 1990s witnessed a political pride in the diversity of Britain, one that has changed significantly since events such as 9/11 and 7/7. There has been a change in the perception of terms such as multi-cultural and cultural diversity, as well as a change in the political usage of the term, and policies have now introduced the notion of "community cohesion" along with a supporting advisory body.[10] The Commission on Integration and Cohesion was charged with the task of supporting local authorities in considering the benefits of an increased diversity in Britain as well as thinking about possible responses to manage tensions and developing approaches to community building.

Cultural diversity in Britain is still a developing field of thought. While the demographic evidence of an immensely diverse population (described by sociologists as a "super-diversity") may state an empirical fact, its interpretation into effective strategies for cultural programming in the arts remains problematic. An all-too-common reading of "culturally diverse" is that of "black minority ethnic," in part a legacy of the "Ethnic Minorities Action Plan," as well as the recognition of the disproportionately low numbers of non-white people participating and working in the mainstream visual arts. While this can translate into specific targets and working principles for arts organisations to change the demographic of their workforce, collections and programming, and can be effective to a degree, there remains a problem with the grammar of this approach.

In understanding "cultural diversity" as describing a portion of society rather than the whole, there is an implication that somehow an invisible "cultural homogeny" can exist, that diversity is only applicable to a certain group of people. This opinion not only creates a separation of "culturally diverse" artists from the mainstream art world but it also creates a dilemma of "over-representation" where a "culturally diverse" artist comes to signify an over-determined idea of difference. Beyond this there are issues of "self-determination," who gets to decide who is "culturally diverse" and who is not? Why can this term be applicable to some and not to others? But these are only a few of the troubling questions of an expanding field.

Our research into this field revealed that many other positions in a landscape of cultural diversity were being occupied, positions that enacted and enabled a landscape to emerge. Some organizations focused more specifically on the cultural diversity within their local area, exploring the histories and cultural interactions of the past as well as the emergent interactions of the future. Others expanded their field of specialization such as the Chinese cultural center, representing the diversity within a specialized field rather than attempting to represent the demographic make up of Manchester. There are alternative interpretations of culture, and numerous other interpretations of cultural diversity that could be mentioned, and these groups are ever shifting, raising the question of whether "diversity is now too diverse" to represent. But one can't help but feel that this would be a disappointing and unsatisfying understanding and "resolution" to the subject of cultural diversity.

It is at this point that Iniva's forthcoming program for "Progress Reports" becomes an active "inquiry" into the representation of cultural diversity in Britain today, considering the changing context for diversity alongside its varying representations; asking questions of diversity and providing a space for our audiences to consider how diversity can take many different shapes in response to changing situations, in brief, an inquiry into the diversity of diversity now.

NOTES

1. The Arts Council of England (previously of Britain) is a major funding body run by the state and operated under the "arm's length principle," meaning that it operates independently of the government despite receiving funding from it.
2. Gavin Jantjes, Towards Cultural Diversity: A Report into the Ethnic Minority Arts Action Plan (Arts Council, London 1989), 1.
3. The Ethnic Minority Arts Action Plan was an Arts Council pledge to commit 4% of its expenditure over 2 years to "Ethnic Minority Arts" to tackle the "under-representation" of people of Afro-Caribbean and Asian descent in the arts. The 4% figure was based on the corresponding percentage of the population.
4. Gavin Jantjes, Towards Cultural Diversity: A Report into the Ethnic Minority Arts Action Plan (Arts Council, London 1989).
5. Originally a group of four artists, Marlene Smith, Donald Rodney, Keith Piper and Eddie Chambers, from the British African-Caribbean community. Immensely innovative and exploratory in mediums and formats (using technology and installation at a time when this was not considered common practice), their work was noted for its boldly political stance, producing dynamic conceptual art that offered a series of inventive critiques on the state of inter-communal, class and gender relations in the UK.
6. Inaugurated in 1982 and dissolved in 1998, the seven-person Black Audio Film Collective (BAFC) is widely acknowledged as one of the most influential artist groups to emerge from Britain in recent years. John Akomfrah, Lina Gopaul, Avril Johnson, Reece Auguiste, Trevor Mathison, David Lawson and Edward George produced award winning film, photography, slide tape, video, installation, posters and interventions, much of which has never been exhibited in Britain.
7. Final Report for the creation of The Institute of New International Visual Arts (INIVA) December 1991, London Arts Board and Arts Council.
8. Iniva was the product of a large body of research by various artists and cultural practioners in collaboration with the Arts council. The research was conducted to determine what was required by those working within the cultural sector as well as to propose an alternative way forward.
9. The Commission on Integration and Cohesion, a fixed term advisory body, was set up to considering how local areas can make the most of the benefits delivered by increasing diversity—and also to consider how they can respond to the tensions it can sometimes cause. It was tasked with developing practical approaches to building communities" own capacity to prevent and manage tensions.

Jessica Harrington is a freelance research associate for Iniva and has recently been working with Iniva to facilitate discussion about the Changing Landscape of cultural diversity in the visual arts.

Iniva engages with new ideas and emerging debates in the contemporary visual arts, reflecting in particular the cultural diversity of contemporary society. We work with artists, curators, creative producers, writers and the public to explore the vitality of visual culture.

Art History Through the Lens of the Present?

Gerald McMaster

The past is never dead. It's not even past.

From Requiem for a Nun, *William Faulkner (1897–1962)*

What has come to be a normal, or natural way of viewing linear art history beginning with some point in the past, advancing to the present, then carrying on into the future, creates problems of presenting certain works of art that sit outside this narrative. What if it was suggested that the past, present, and future are always present within us and that all three enlighten and influence our experience of the present? A strictly linear art history that begins in the late 18th century in eastern Canada and progressed up to the present would not allow us to see our land and our history in a new way. Indeed, a traditional view of Canada would not get us far in re-examining our history, if we were unable to view it from the present; and it is from the present that the Art Gallery of Ontario views its newly reinstalled McLean Centre for Canadian Art.

The idea of seeing the collection in a new way comes at a time in our history in which we are re-examining who we are. This strategy was developed as part of the institution's new mission for a new building program. With the new building, the idea of Transformation AGO was born. With the new slogan — new building, new ideas, new future — was born the opportunity to begin anew. With a new building program led by Frank Gehry,[1] coupled with one of the country's finest art collections, it was indeed the critical opening to consider new ways of seeing the collection. We were able to consider abandoning the traditional view of the "chronological hang," which presents art as a series of discrete movements, styles, or "isms." Instead, the collection was reinvigorated by drawing upon the idea that we can see art in new ways through explorations of overarching themes. In other words, there are different ways of viewing art, and the new presentations enabled visitors to ask new questions.

Journal of Museum Education, Volume 34, Number 3, Fall 2009, pp. 215–222.

"Mythmakers and Meaning Seekers," Molly and George Gilmour Gallery, Art Gallery of Ontario, *©Art Gallery of Ontario 2009.*

In addition, a few other factors must be considered. First, we recognized the indispensable participation of the visitor to the gallery, and thus the viewer of the work, without whom the artwork is nothing, just a dead object. By refocusing on the visitor, we felt the art and thus the space would come alive. This relationship was laid out in the institution's six guiding principles: diversity, relevance, forum, creativity, responsiveness, and transparency. Next, we were wholly aware of the changing times. How? By understanding that the diversity and complexity of our time requires many voices; as well, by interrogating various representations, we maintain that we will get to understand new ways of seeing, which in turn will take visitors to new levels of self-awareness and toward a diversity of voices. Finally, constructing the galleries along thematic ideas enabled us to examine various "narratives" (the "silenced voices"), in new ways, such as women and First Nations; and, by examining and making public the thematic ideas inherent in the objects, many new and distinct voices could be engaged to read the works and thus engender new and relevant connections.

Since our memories/stories are anchored in diverse material (art) objects, we asked additional questions: How can our research into specific works, or the space between the works, be helpful to the visitor trying to understand the complexity of Canadian art? History allows communities to renew and remember themselves and traditions; sometimes this creates negative situations where there is a resistance to outside influence and perhaps a negation of traditional stories. The stories—the histories/issues—hold power, not only for knowing the past, but also positioning those who hear them within a larger context. The stories we want to tell have multiple meanings and values that need to be told within a community. Looking at art objects today through interdisciplinary approaches, where there is more than one authority, can provide new and fresh perspectives.

Our first consideration for the re-hang was to recognize that Canada has a visual art history predating the arrival of Europeans. With this new introduction, we effectively shifted the traditional view of the start of Canadian art. The first Canadian gallery that visitors enter at the AGO is filled with a thousand projectile points—arrowheads, spear points, and knives. Fewer than half are small fully-formed points dating from 1,000 to 11,000 years ago; they sit on one wall. On the other wall, more than half are half-formed, in other words, they may have been discarded or not yet fully shaped. They appear as an art installation, in an art gallery, not an ethnographic or archaeological museum, although we worked with an archaeologist. During the

A thousand points for a thousand generations—installation of projectile points with curator Gerald McMaster on video, Bovey Gallery, Art Gallery of Ontario. *©Art Gallery of Ontario 2009.*

gestation period for this exhibit, internal debates were exchanged about the worth of these "points" as art objects; the decision in the end was to carry the idea through to its logical end. The debates prompted us to bring various voices together—an art historian, a contemporary art curator, an archaeologist, a First Nations carver, an art student, an 8-year-old, a First Nations elder and tribal leader. The voices were both Francophone and Anglophone and all were asked the same question: Are these works of art? The idea was to bring the argument out into the public realm; in other words, we had to have some level of transparency with our own debates.

My background as an artist and curator of historic and contemporary First Nations art considered through the lens of cultural analysis, theory, and interpretation, combined with a very smart team of young curators, allowed us to decide upon an approach to Canadian art that was different from the received historical practice as previously outlined. In presenting the historical Canadian collection to the public, our aim is to understand how these works are a critical part of the present; how do they live with us, and how do we live with them? History is always around us and we seem to live with it. Thus, reading the past through the lens of the present brings it closer to the first person, bringing life to the work. By doing so, it allows us to use the collection in interesting ways. As historians who focus on popular memory have insisted, we experience the present through the lens of the past—and we shape our understanding of the past through the lens of the present. Thus, examining and presenting projectile points in an art gallery becomes a pivotal point for the new AGO.

The new Canadian Wing is organized thematically, under "memory," "myth," and "power." For example, one of the galleries, called "Ancient Memory," explores the ways in which memories are recorded as a means of marking our place, our time, and our events. Questions guiding curatorial thinking were: How does the past shape the present and how do we examine the past through a contemporary lens? How have we tried to erase ancient memory? How has art preserved these memories? In this gallery, we sought to understand the ancient history of Aboriginal peoples through their art over the past millennia and longer.

In presenting the new Canadian galleries with the intention of viewing the past through the lens of the present, we walk the fine line of being criticized for "present-ism." But looking at the past in this way is inescapable; there are many attendant issues of the approach that must be acknowledged. Historical examination is, of course full of contradictions, points of view,

Drawstring pouch, (around 1720), Anishnaabe artist, Great Lakes region and *The West Wind (winter 1916–1917)* by Tom Thomson (1877–1917) Gift of the Canadian Club of Toronto, Art Gallery of Ontario. ©Art Gallery of Ontario 2009.

and so on. There could have been more ways we might have examined the past, but we believe that what we chose was most appropriate for what we eventually settled upon. Unlike the past, why can we not reread history? We can't undo the past; we can, rewrite the past, and revise it; however, it can't be undone.

In another gallery, for example, we have one of Canada's most iconic works, *The West Wind,* by Tom Thomson. It is sandwiched between Emily Carr's equally enduring *Indian Church,* and two late-18th century Anishnaabe pouches. At one time in history, the two paintings would have been admired as important signifiers along carefully articulated historical developments. There is no denying this story. But the in the new AGO, the emphasis has shifted slightly. The three works now speak of the enduring power of myth in guiding how we view the world. As well, the juxtapositioning of *The West Wind* with the Anishnaabe (First Nation) pouches carefully suggests a new way of looking. In this instance, both look at the northern landscape of Ontario: one through Western eyes, the other through Anishnaabe eyes.

Today, the many stories (narratives) we tell can be considered neither true nor false, just like these two works: one work tells of a new landscape, while the other says it's ancient. Myth is beyond science, it embodies in symbol and narrative a vision of reality. Some speak about ancient times that explain why the world is the way it is. These stories function as rationalizations for the fundamental mysteries of life.

Prior to scientific discourse, societies all over the world devised narratives of creation, resurrection, and complex systems of supernatural beings, each with specific powers, and stories about their actions. Throughout the world, myths provide people with explanations, histories, role models, entertainment, and many other things that enable them to direct their own actions and understand their own surroundings. Canadian artists from various times and cultures have been inspired by myths and have given them visual form. In many cases, works of art are the only surviving reflection of what particular cultures believed and valued. But even where written records or oral traditions exist, art adds to our understanding of myths. Many narratives are so compelling that artists have turned to them again and again, reinterpreting them from the vantage point of their own experience and imagination.

Indeed, isn't history nearly always in a state of being rewritten or recomposed? Isn't this the beauty and the joy and the challenge of writing history? Jon Christensen says, "Unlike the past, which is, well, past, history is always in the present." Today, some of the best, most engaging history is an argument aimed at the heart and soul of the present. George Herbert Mead (1863–1931), American philosopher and social theorist, argues that the historical past, insofar as it is capable of being experienced, is transformed by novel events. History is not written on an unchanging scroll. Novelty gives the lie to this way of seeing the past. By virtue of its originality, the novel event can not be explained or understood in terms of prior interpretations of the past. The past, which by definition can only exist in the present, changes to "conform" to novel events (James 1890, 237–283).

Proceeding through the galleries, we come across a work by a contemporary artist of Aboriginal ancestry, Kent Monkman, with his over-sized painting called *The Academy*. Commissioned for the reopening of the AGO, it sits within a gallery of largely historical works. The artist took as his inspiration a number of works from the AGO permanent collection and those situated in the same gallery, along with his fascination with the works of American artist George Catlin. Thus, it appears as a history painting within a history gallery. The interventionist strategy of this work brings to life the much older works. Suddenly visitors are confronted with historical issues by a contemporary artist and connections are immediately made with the many disparate works around it. Monkman wove together various intersecting

The Academy by Kent Monkman (1965–), 2008, acrylic on canvas, Art Gallery of Ontario. Purchased with the assistance of the David Yuile and Mary Elizabeth Hodgson Fund, 2008. *©Art Gallery of Ontario 2009.*

stories to the extent that it has been one of the most popular works in the Canadian Wing for its interpretive promise.

CONCLUSION

Art functions as a recorder and catalyst for reflection and dialogue about the dynamics of power that affects human lives. The new installation in the Canadian Wing encourages visitor exploration and personalization into various aspects of power, myth, and memory, using the artworks as catalysts, provocations, and points of creative reflection. Power struggles and relations are universal, complex, and dynamic. They exist across all social, cultural, and political lines, and historically they have been documented and reflected through art.

The AGO took the opportunity to change history by reinstalling or rehanging the Canadian Wing. Kathy Halbreich, the former Walker Art Center Director, says:

> …re-hangs are about re-seeing, [they are about] breaking down old ideas about how, and in what context, art should be seen. It's both

stimulating and clarifying either to create new or abandon old hierarchies, to disrupt preconceived notions of, say, beauty, or to fiddle with the drama of the space itself."

The public, especially the local community, now gets to see more of the collection, especially familiar works. As we now begin programming for the future, we will be able to show more of the collection in frequently-changing rooms. Without losing sight of the thematic approach, we believe that visitors will approach the collection in new ways; they will begin to grasp First Nation aesthetics, or they may have greater awareness of contributions by women artists. We feel that with our ever-growing and complex nation, coupled with our ever-growing and complex collection, we have had to find new and powerful ways of address, ones that are seen and heard through many voices.

Note

1. The Art Gallery of Ontario reopened in November 2008 in the new Frank Gehry-designed building, located in the heart of Toronto's Chinatown; it is situated in the neighbourhood of Gehry's birth.

References

Christensen, Jon, "Down in the valley: A call to undo the dam at Hetch Hetchy," Review, San Francisco Chronicle, Sunday, October 23, 2005.
James, William. The Principles of Psychology, Volume One. New York: Henry Holt & Co., 1890. Reprinted, New York: Dover Publications, 1950.

Gerald McMaster is the Fredrik S. Eaton Curator, Canadian Art at the Art Gallery of Ontario. Before joining the AGO, McMaster worked with the Smithsonian's National Museum of the American Indian, where he was deputy assistant director for cultural resources and later responsible for design and content of three permanent exhibitions. He previously worked as curator of contemporary art at the Canadian Museum of Civilization, and later as curator in charge of First People's Hall. Originally from Saskatchewan. He is a leading authority on First Nations art in Canada and recipient of the 2005 National Aboriginal Achievement Award and the Order of Canada.

Access Is Not a Text Alternative

Stephen Brown

Abstract   Museums and other heritage institutions have a duty in most cases to make their contents and services as widely available, relevant, and usable as is reasonably possible. Web delivery can help by making it possible to access content and services in locations and at times more convenient to the individual: internet access in the home/internet café/public library, mobile phones, hand held PDAs, podcasts on MP3 players etc. although there are of course digital divide issues. But access is not the same as accessibility. Accessibility refers to the ease with which a wide range of users, including those with disabilities of various kinds, can use the content and services on offer. Despite legislation in many countries making accessibility a legal requirement, many museum Web sites, including those of leading national institutions, fall short of the principle of equality of experience for all users. Possible reasons for this are complex: lack of awareness and understanding, time, skills and know-how. This paper focuses on two of these: understanding and know-how, discussing the limitations of current technology-focused guidelines and describes a set of heuristics based on a holistic human-centred approach, that are simultaneously more manageable and yet more inclusive. These "rules of thumb" can be quickly and easily implemented using simple, readily available, and free tools and techniques to assess the accessibility of Web site designs.

Museums and other heritage institutions generally have a commission to make their contents and services as widely available, relevant, and usable as is reasonably possible in pursuit of such goals as supporting lifelong learning, building cultural understanding, creating a climate of inclusion, and encouraging social cohesion (Lawley 2003, Sandell 2003). In the UK, museums are required to present evidence of their performance in relation to these

Journal of Museum Education, Volume 34, Number 3, Fall 2009, pp. 223–234.

goals (Hooper-Greenhill 2004) and funding is contingent on being able to present such evidence (Selwood 2001). While the UK funding environment may be unusually explicit in this regard, due to the direct and extensive investment of tax revenues in heritage institutions in that country, it would not be surprising if funding agencies elsewhere have similar expectations of a return on investment in social and cultural capital.

Web delivery can help by making it possible for people to access museum content and services in locations, and at times more convenient to them, via, for example, internet access at home, internet café, public library, mobile phones, handheld PDAs, podcasts on MP3 players, etc. As the cost of access falls and the availability and bandwidth of connections increases, the ideal of universal remote access becomes more feasible, with obvious implications for museums.

With the number of UK households and small businesses adopting broadband now passing the three million mark, museums need to consider the approaches they can use to present curator's expertise to new audiences in engaging ways for broadband (Blyth 2005).

Many museums have already responded enthusiastically to this challenge. In 2001, the UK Museums Libraries and Archives Council (MLA) noted that:

> Museums are being reinvented as physical and virtual spaces in which people engage and learn, interacting with objects, and discovering their stories. Interweaving the real and the virtual creates a powerful brand, enabling museums to occupy centre stage in cultural cyberspace (MLA 2001).

There are, of course, issues around equality of access. Internet access is still not universal in such advanced industrialized nations such as the United States, Australia, the UK, and other western European Union members, let alone in developing nations. In 2007, the UK Department of Culture Media and Sport (DCMS) noted:

> Although disparities in home internet access between the lowest and the highest income groups have narrowed, those living in the highest income group are still seven times more likely to have access to the Internet (Hutton 2007).

However, although they are important, these digital divide issues are a potential distraction from our main focus here because access is not the same thing as accessibility. While access is about being able to tap into networks, accessibility refers to the ease with which a wide range of users, including those with disabilities of various kinds, can use the content and services on offer via those networks. Online accessibility is therefore clearly predicated on Internet access but goes beyond mere access to the resource to address broader issues of its usability.

ACCESSIBILITY AND MUSEUM WEB SITES

Many countries have enacted legislation that makes it illegal to discriminate against a disabled person by refusing to provide a service if it is already provided to the general public, or by making it impossible or unreasonably difficult for a disabled person to make use of any service. The UK Disability Discrimination Act 1995 (http://www.opsi.gov.uk/acts/acts1995/Ukpga_19950050_en_1.htm), section 508 of the US Rehabilitation Act (http://www.access-board.gov/sec508/guide/act.htm), and the Disability Discrimination Act 1992 in Australia (http://scaleplus.law.gov.au/html/pasteact/0/311/top.htm) are just some examples. Yet despite such legislation, many museum Web sites, including those of leading national institutions fall short of the principle of equality of experience for all users. A recent international survey of 125 museum Web sites revealed that the level of accessibility of such sites is not high. Only 30% of English museum sites and 20% of those from other countries passed a basic technical test of accessibility, and user trials found that visually and cognitively impaired users could successfully complete only 75% of very basic tasks such as finding museum opening hours and facilities for disabled users. A third of the study's test users felt lost on at least one occasion and completely blind people in particular found the sites difficult to use (Petrie et al 2005). These findings prompt two questions:

1. How is it that only 20–30% of these sites passed basic technical accessibility tests when disabled users could in fact successfully complete 75% of at least very basic tasks on those sites? Are technical tests a reliable guide to real user usability?

2. How can museum Web site accessibility be improved?

The remainder of this paper attempts to answer these questions, with particular emphasis on accessibility.

The World Wide Web Consortium (W3C), which is responsible for the coordination of Web standards has taken a lead in promoting accessibility of the Web for disabled people. Since 1997, its Web Accessibility Initiative (WAI) has worked to raise awareness of the importance of Web accessibility internationally and promoted its own Web Content Accessibility Guidelines (WCAG) (W3C, 1999; W3C, 2008).

The WAI model and the original WCAG guidelines (version 1.0) have been criticized for their technology focus. WCAG 1.0 was HTML specific, with few references to newer technologies such as CSS and JavaScript (Kelly et al 2005). Consequently most of the guidelines are valid only for the simplest Web sites today. This probably explains why such a high proportion of Web sites fail technical accessibility tests based on WCAG 1.0 but perform better on tests involving real users. Nevertheless this does not excuse the residual 25% failure rate of such trials, especially when we consider that this failure rate refers to very basic navigation and information retrieval tasks, that a third of the study's test users felt lost on at least one occasion, and completely blind people, in particular, found the sites difficult to use.

Clearly there is more to successful Web site design than slavish adherence to WCAG 1.0 (Kelly et al 2009). What is needed perhaps is a not only a set of guidelines that are technology neutral, but practical guidance for Web developers to help them apply the guidelines quickly and easily to real Web designs. The latest version of WCAG (version 2.0) published in December 2008 places the onus on the developer to ensure that whatever technologies they employ are known to be supported rather than tying developers to specific technologies. But that still leaves the issue of practical guidance.

TESTS FOR ACCESSIBILITY

We have already seen that technical accessibility tests may not be wholly reliable. A further limitation is that while they help you to check an existing site for accessibility errors, they cannot offer guidance on how to build a site, other than retrospectively, i.e., "this doesn't work" or "this is fine." Thompson et al (2003) suggested a list of practical checks, based on WCAG 1.0, that can be used during Web development to check site usability. The advantage of this kind of checklist is that it prompts designers to think about what they should or should not do, as well as suggesting ways of testing the results. What follows is a reinterpretation of the Thompson et al. Checklist, updated to take account of WCAG 2.0 guidelines.

1. Turn off browser images and see if the graphics have text equivalents (WCAG 1.0: 1.1, WCAG 2.0:1.1).

2. If the page contains audio content, ensure that a text equivalent is available (WCAG 1.0: 1.1, WCAG 2.0: 1.1. / 1.2).

3. Change the font size (if possible) and assess if the page is still readable (WCAG 1.0): 3.1 / 3.3 / 3.4, WCAG 2.0: 1.3 / 1.4).

4. View the page at a screen resolution of 640 x 480 pixels and assess if the information contained is still accessible (WCAG 1.0: none, WCAG 2.0: 1.3).

5. Examine use of colour. Is it used exclusively to convey information? If inadequate colour contrast is suspected, investigate this by printing the page, or "grab" the screen in question and "desaturate" the colour from it using a paint package (WCAG 1.0: 2.1, WCAG 2.0: 1.3).

6. Tab through the page to see if all links / form controls are accessible without a mouse (WCAG 1.0: 9.4, WCAG 2.0: 2.1).

7. Use Jaws or an equivalent screen reader and observe if the information contained within the page is still available. (The free Firefox screen reader emulation software Fangs, available at: http://sourceforge.net/projects/fangs/ is a useful substitute.) Also, note if a "skip navigation" link is present to speed up use with a screen reader (WCAG 1.0: 1.1 and 5, WCAG 2.0: 1.4 / 2.4). (Thompson et al 2003)

Figures 1 and 2 show an example of poor navigation layout revealed by the use of a screen reader. In Figure 1, the map contains hotspots that link to individual photographic and text descriptions of specific locations on the map. Users wishing to skip the maps and go straight to these more detailed records can follow the link at the bottom of the screen to see "all the results from this map." To a normally sighted reader, this layout makes sense. The interactive map is there to explore, but immediately below it is a short cut to the underlying data. By contrast, Figure 2 shows how this same screen appears to anyone using a screen reader. Screen readers work methodically through all the text from the top to the bottom of the screen. Notice how much meaningless content (the text version of the map image) the user would have to listen to before they reached the "handy" shortcut to "all the results from this map."

In addition four further checks have been added to the Thompson et al. original checklist to cover dynamic content and equivalence of content.

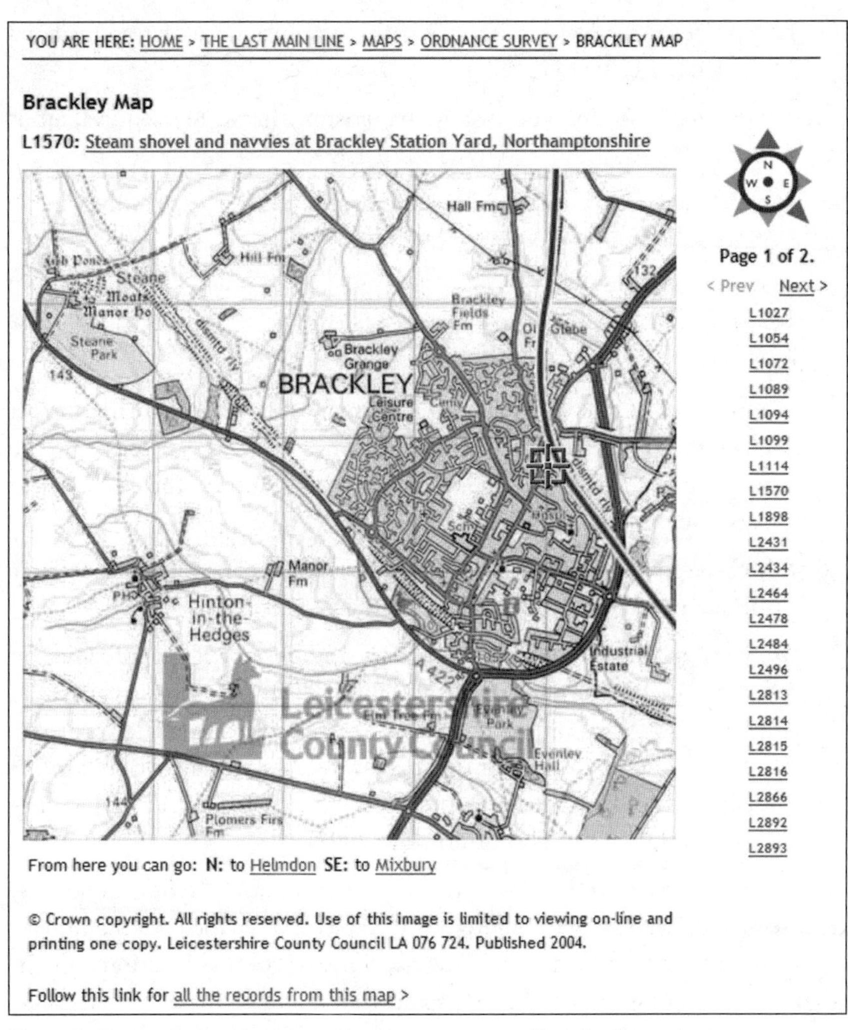

Figure 1. Interactive map screen as it appears to normally sighted people.

1. Check whether understanding and use of the page is dependent on running any scripts and whether any alternatives to scripts are provided (WCAG 1.): 6.3. WCAG 2.): 1.1 / 1.2). Scripting can add useful interactive functions such as the hotspot cursors linked to further information in Figure 1. But scripts can also reduce accessibility and confuse assistive technologies such as screen readers. Dynamic drop-down menus in particular are known to cause significant accessibility problems for people with motor or visual impairments, for example when screen magnifiers are used. To find out if a page is running scripts right click on it and

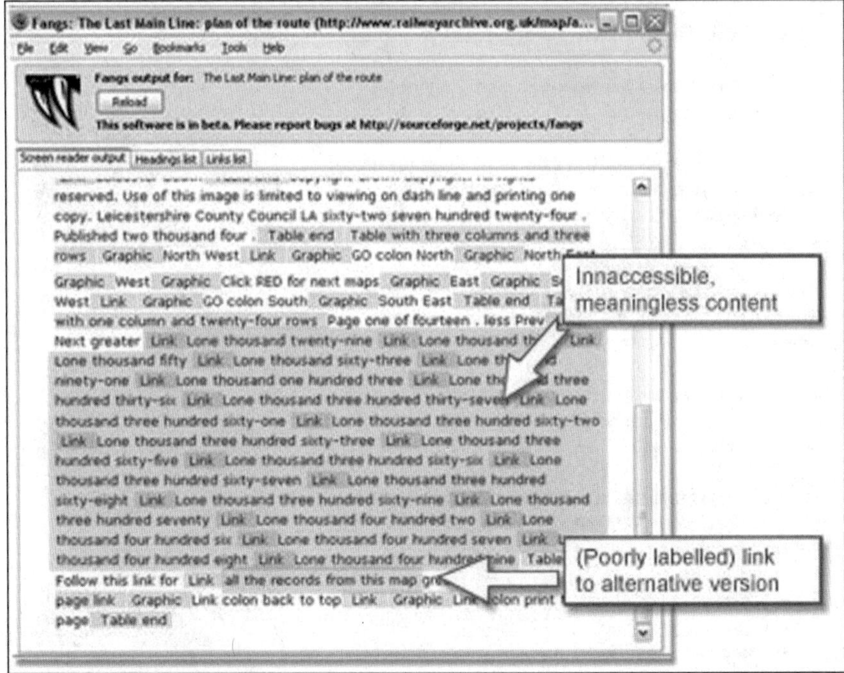

Figure 2. The same screen showing how a screen reader reveals the poorly positioned link to alternative text.

```
<!DOCTYPE html PUBLIC "-//W3C//DTD XHTML 1.0 Strict//EN" "http://www.w3.org/TR/xhtml1/DTD/xhtml1-strict.dtd">
<html xmlns="http://www.w3.org/1999/xhtml" xml:lang="en" lang="en">
        <head>
                <title>The Last Main Line: plan of the route</title>
                <meta http-equiv="Content-Type" content="text/html; charset=iso-8859-1" />

                <meta http-equiv="content-style-type" content="text/css" />
                <meta http-equiv="content-language" content="en-GB" />
                <meta name="keywords" content="Great Central Railway route plan map chart ordnance survey last main line tran
                <meta name="description" content="The plan of the Great Central Railway (below) shows construction contracts,
                <meta name="robots" content="index, follow" />


                <link href="/stylesheets/raiPage.css" rel="stylesheet" title="railstylesheet" />

                <script type="text/javascript" src="/javascript/rollover.js"></script>
                <script type="text/javascript" src="/javascript/subNav.js"></script>          scripting

                <script type="text/javascript">
                <!--
                        var linkName;

                        function mapLink_onmouseover(idNo, xRef, yRef, linkNameIn, refNum, recordText)
                        {
                                var smLinkID = "link" + idNo;
                                var refTitle = document.getElementById("titleCell");

                                refTitle.innerHTML = '<strong>' + refNum + ': <a href="getobjectmap.php' + linkNameIn + '">'
```

Figure 3. An example of embedded script

select "view source". Figure 3 shows what the scripting for the interactive map shown in Figure 1 looks like.

2. Check to see if scripts are dependent upon "device-specific event-handlers" such as mouse clicks and movements (WCAG 1.0: 6.4, WCAG 2.0: 2.1). Users who do not and/or cannot use such devices are disadvantaged if a site has been designed with dependence on specific device

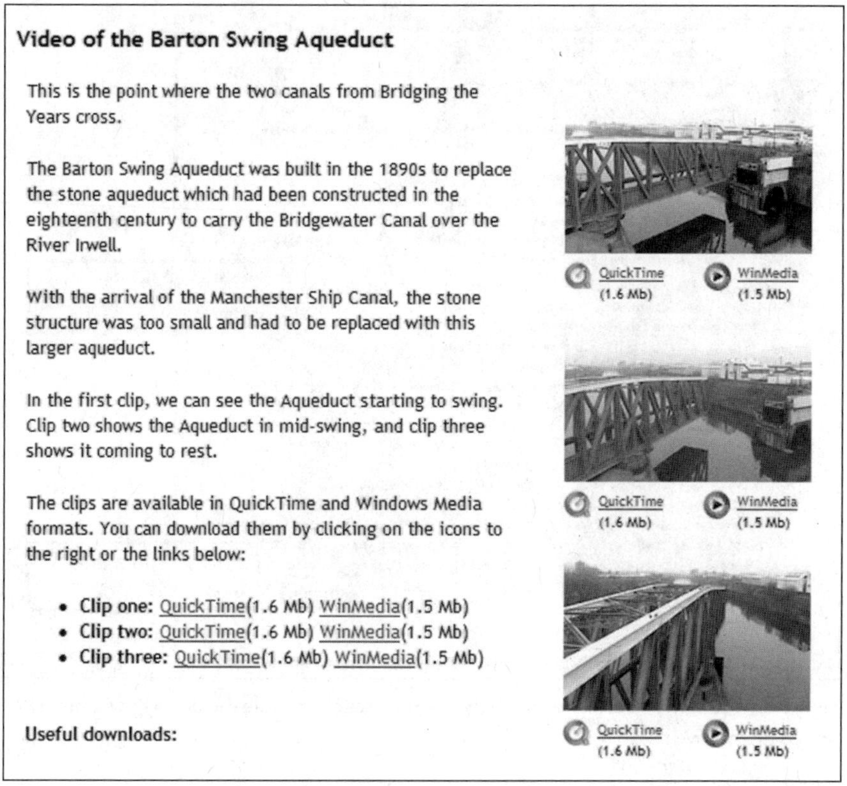

Video of the Barton Swing Aqueduct

This is the point where the two canals from Bridging the Years cross.

The Barton Swing Aqueduct was built in the 1890s to replace the stone aqueduct which had been constructed in the eighteenth century to carry the Bridgewater Canal over the River Irwell.

With the arrival of the Manchester Ship Canal, the stone structure was too small and had to be replaced with this larger aqueduct.

In the first clip, we can see the Aqueduct starting to swing. Clip two shows the Aqueduct in mid-swing, and clip three shows it coming to rest.

The clips are available in QuickTime and Windows Media formats. You can download them by clicking on the icons to the right or the links below:

- **Clip one:** QuickTime(1.6 Mb) WinMedia(1.5 Mb)
- **Clip two:** QuickTime(1.6 Mb) WinMedia(1.5 Mb)
- **Clip three:** QuickTime(1.6 Mb) WinMedia(1.5 Mb)

Useful downloads:

QuickTime (1.6 Mb)   WinMedia (1.5 Mb)

QuickTime (1.6 Mb)   WinMedia (1.5 Mb)

QuickTime (1.6 Mb)   WinMedia (1.5 Mb)

Figure 4. Text description of video content.

types (such as a mouse for navigation). To test for this, try navigating around the site using only the keyboard.

3. If the page contains video content, ensure that a text equivalent is available (WCAG 1.0: 1.1, WCAG 2.0: 1.1. / 1.2). Figure 4 shows a page that attempts to describe as closely as possible what is shown in the videos on the page.

4. Check to see if text equivalents are truly equivalent or do they leave out information that is contained in the multimedia element (perhaps image, sound, etc.) that is essential to its understanding? (WCAG 1.0: 1.1, WCAG 2.0: 1.1. / 1.2). Is a version of the video offered with an audio description? Audio description provides an extra narrative voice that describes what the user would observe if they could see the presentation clearly (WCAG 1.0: 1.1, WCAG 2.0: 1.1. / 1.2). Figure 5 shows an attempt to provide a range of alternative experiences using different media.

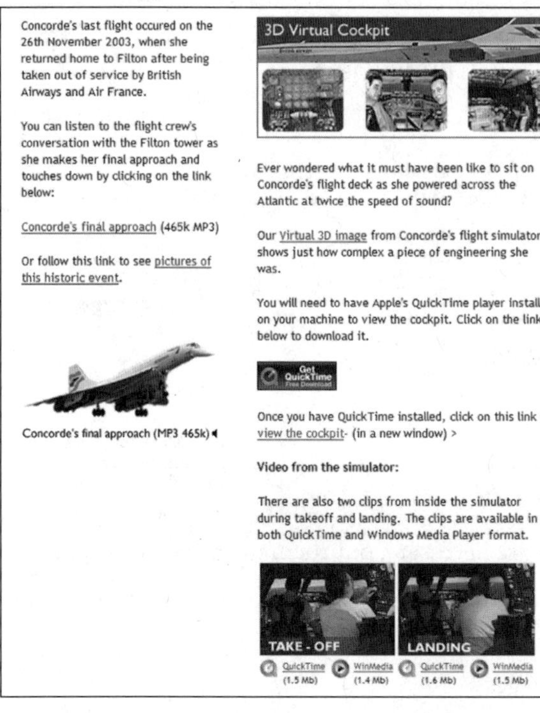

Figure 5. A range of alternative media used to provide similar experiences.

ACCESSIBILITY TIPS

The examples cited above were reported more fully in Brown and Gerrard (2006), a comparative study of the Transport Archive site, from which the above illustrations were taken, and an online exhibition about the modern world created by the UK National Museum of Science and Industry. These sites were selected for analysis because they are both award winners and thus models of good practice. Yet, despite this, a number of accessibility problems were identified with each when the tests suggested here were applied. These accessibility tests can be applied during Web site development to check for adherence to best practice, but obviously require some content to have been developed first. The WCAG guidelines were developed originally to help designers to avoid common accessibility pitfalls. But not everyone is familiar with WCAG or finds them easy to use. The following checklist of accessibility tips is offered as a simplified introduction to the basic provisions of the guidelines:

1. Any single medium will be inaccessible to some people, so provide alternatives and not just a text alternative.

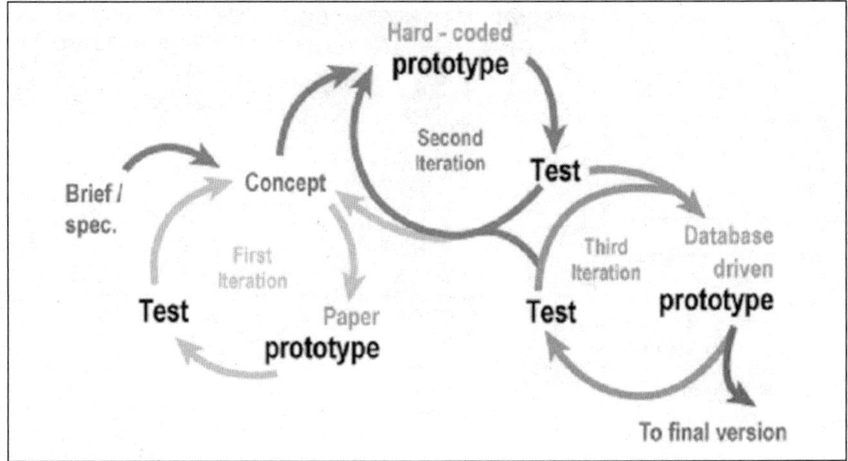

Figure 6. Test your ideas early and often.

1. If "alternative versions" are necessary, put them in an accessible place.

2. Don't make media elements hard to access by embedding one inside another.

3. Don't format text as images.

4. Synchronize video text captions or audio descriptions with the video itself.

5. Sites that offer alternative routes and media work well for everyone, not just those with accessibility requirements.

6. Test your designs on real users as early and as often as possible to find out how they really work, don't just rely on technical accessibility tests or your own ability to make the site work (after all, you know it too well to see its shortcomings).

CONCLUSIONS

Access is not the same as accessibility. Access is about being able to get to the resource. Accessibility is about being able to use it. Despite the availability of accessibility guidelines and the potential threat of legal and financial sanctions, many museum Web sites have fallen short of offering equivalent experiences to users with varying abilities. It seems unlikely that lack of awareness of the importance of accessibility is a major cause. Lack of understanding of what accessibility guidelines mean and lack of knowledge about how to apply them effectively seem more likely candidates. This paper has argued that W3C guidelines have been difficult to interpret and automated technical accessibility tests have not always been a reliable guide to usability. To overcome these limitations, a simplified set of accessibility principles is offered and a battery of tests is suggested that can be quickly and easily implemented using simple, readily available, and free tools and techniques to assess the accessibility of Web site designs.

Acknowledgments

This paper is an abridged and revised version of Brown S. and Gerrard D. (2006) Squaring the Triangle: The Implications of Broadband for Access, Diversity and Accessibility published March 1, 2006 at http://www.archimuse.com/mw2006/papers/brown/brown.html

References

Blyth, T. (2005) Curating for Broadband. In D. Bearman and J. Trant (eds.). *Museums and the Web, Selected papers from Museums and the Web 2005*. Toronto: Archives and Museum Informatics 205–212.

Brown S. and Gerrard D. (2006) "Squaring the Triangle: The Implications of Broadband for Access, Diversity and Accessibility in Museum Web Design," in J. Trant and D. Bearman (eds.). *Museums and the Web 2006: Proceedings,* Toronto: Archives & Museum Informatics, 47-57, published March 1, 2006 at http://www.archimuse.com/mw2006/papers/brown/brown.html. Accessed 14/09/2009.

Hooper-Greenhill, E. (2004) Measuring Learning Outcomes in Museums, Archives and Libraries: The Learning Impact Research Project (LIRP). *International Journal of Heritage Studies,* 10(2) 151–174.

Hutton, W. (2007) *Staying Ahead: the economic performance of the UK's creative industries.* London: The Work Foundation/Department of Culture, Media and Sport. http://www.culture.gov.uk/reference_library/publications/3672.aspx/ Accessed 14/10/09.

Kelly, B., Sloan, D., Phipps, L. Petrie, H., & Hamilton, F. (2005) Forcing standardization or accommodating diversity? A framework for applying the WCAG in the real world. *Proceedings of the 2005 International Cross-Disciplinary Workshop on Web Accessibility (W4A),* pp. 46–54. New York: ACM Press http://www.ukoln.ac.uk/web-focus/papers/w4a-2005/ Accessed 14/09/2009.

Kelley, B., Sloan, D. Brown, S., Seale, J., Lauke, P., Ball, S., & Smith, S. (2009) Accessibility 2.0: Next Steps for Web Accessibility. *Journal of Access Services,* 6; 265–294.

Lawley, I. (2003) Local authority museums and the modernizing government agenda in England. Museum and Society, 1(2) 75-86.

MLA (2001) *Renaissance in the Regions. Executive Summary of the Regional Museums Task Force Report* http://www.mla.gov.uk/action/regional/ren_es.asp Accessed 7/01/06.

Petrie H., King N. and Weisen M. (2005) The Accessibility of Museum Web sites: results from an English investigation and international comparisons. In D. Bearman and J. Trant (eds): *Museums and the Web 2005: Proceedings.* Toronto: Archives and Museum Informatics, 2005. http://www.archimuse.com/mw2005/papers/petrie/petrie.html Accessed 14/09/2009.

Sandell, R. (2003) Social inclusion, the museum and the dynamics of sectoral change. *Museum and Society*, 1 (1) 45-62.
Selwood, S. (ed) (2001). *The UK cultural sector: profile and policy issues*. Cultural Trends and Policy Studies Institute, London.
Thompson T., Burgstahler S. and Comden D. (2003) Research on Web Accessibility in Higher Education. *Information Technology and Disability*, 9 (2) December 2003 http://www.rit.edu/~easi/itd/itdv09n2/thompson.htm Accessed 16/12/05.
W3C (1999) *Web content accessibility guidelines 1.0*. http://www.w3.org/TR/WCAG10/ Accessed 14/09/2009.
W3C (2008) *Web content accessibility guidelines 2.0*. http://www.w3.org/TR/WCAG/ Accessed 14/09/2009.

Stephen Brown is Professor of Learning Technologies and Director of Knowledge Media Design at De Montfort University, UK (http://kmd.dmu.ac.uk) and Visiting Fellow, Centre for Distance Education, University of London. His career includes course design, research and tutoring for the Open University; Head of Distance Learning at BT; Royal Academy of Engineering Visiting Professor in Engineering Design; Director of the International Institute for Electronic Library Research, De Montfort University; Senior Technology Adviser to the JISC; and President of the Association for Learning Technology.

Walking with Janet Cardiff, Sitting with Massimo Guerrera, and Eating Apples with R. Murray Schafer
Meaningful Museum Experiences with Participatory Art for Visitors with and without Visual Impairments

Elizabeth Sweeney

Abstract   As Anthony Robbins once said "If you do what you have always done, you will get what you have always got." Now more than ever museums and galleries are seeking to attract new audiences and find innovative and meaningful ways to engage visitors. While these institutions aim to respond to their responsibility to provide access to their collections, new modes of interpretation are needed to ensure they reach a wider audience. This audience must include the ever-growing population of visitors with disabilities, who for too long have been denied their human right to cultural heritage. When it comes to visitors who are blind or partially sighted, many art galleries are left scrambling to find ways to provide quality programming and access to their all too often "untouchable" art collections. Unfortunately, sometimes this means that visitors with visual impairments are segregated for specialized programming, isolating them from their sighted friends and family members. This article will provide examples of how The National Gallery of Canada has adapted public programs and developed new ways for diverse audiences of various ages and abilities to come together in inclusive settings. Furthermore it will explore how interactive and participatory art can be instrumental in providing meaningful museum experiences and opportunities for multisensory engagement, which in turn offer an entry point for new visitors. Visitors do not require a PhD in art history to "get it," they need simply to show up and participate. What is notable here is that these experiences are not watered down or simplified—in fact the contrary. The outcomes of these programs and exhibitions suggest that

Journal of Museum Education, Volume 34, Number 3, Fall 2009, pp. 235-248.

> visitors are looking for challenges and opportunities to engage with art, in ways they have never tried before, even if it's hard.

"Art is more than what we see."
Penny Leclair, Deaf-blind visitor [1]

PLEASE DO NOT TOUCH THE ARTWORK.

It's the museum security guard mantra, virtually the world over. Anyone who has been to or worked in a museum will be familiar with this rule. Such notices exist, because visitors have a tendency to want to do just that, touch. This desire is certainly understandable considering that recent studies in cognitive psychology have concluded that we actually learn more, when we are able to touch that which we are looking at and hearing about.[2] When multiple senses are engaged we learn more than when only one sense is stimulated.[3] For visitors with visual impairments, having an opportunity to learn using senses other then sight, is not just desirable, it's essential.

When museums offer new methods of engagement through a multi-sensory approach, they in turn provide more opportunities for a wider audience to participate, which promotes greater access to collections. This can be achieved by developing multi-modal learning opportunities that not only allow visitors to touch, but also create the opportunity for meaningful experiences which allow visitors to engage both with an artwork and with each other. By doing this we, in short, provide new ways for our visitors to 'get it'. In an attempt to respond to how museums can diversify their audiences, this article will explore examples of museum programs and exhibitions at the Na-

Penny, a Deaf-blind visitor discusses her perspective on art in Stimulating the Senses. *Photo © NGC*

tional Gallery of Canada that promote multi-modal learning opportunities, for both visitors with and without visual impairments.

ART FOR ALL

The National Gallery of Canada has been delivering adapted programs for visitors with disabilities in some capacity for over 20 years. The Gallery was fortunate to have received support from The J.W. McConnell Family Foundation to develop education and public programs for visitors with disabilities. This included hiring an accessibility educator (myself) for a 3-year term to research, develop and implement new programs while adapting and expanding existing ones, as well as creating local and national partnerships. Unlike many major museums in the US and the UK, (e.g., Metropolitan Museum of Art, the Museum of Modern Art (NY), Victoria and Albert, etc.) where designated accessibility coordinators are standard fixtures, it is speculated that this was the first time in Canada one employee had been assigned the singular responsibility of researching and ensuring access for Deaf and disabled visitors through public programming.

These programs, affectionately called Art for All, were the result of initial research and mentorship from international leaders such as the museums mentioned above, the Tate Modern in London, as well as the powerhouse Art Education for the Blind in New York. Most importantly, Art for All is sustained and dependant on an advisory committee, which comprises of self-advocates with disabilities, special education teachers, mental health professionals, art educators and support workers. The committee meets periodically as a group and members are called upon individually for specific consultation and to provide gallery staff training. This committee offers an essential connection with the community and from it many partnerships and collaborations resulted. One example of this is an ongoing partnership with Family Services à la famille Ottawa, whose staff became actively involved in the advisory committee. This committee member offered extensive training to gallery staff on strategies for working with adults living with mental illness and collaborated in the development of workshops for his clients. In turn, when Family Services à la famille Ottawa wanted to offer their staff professional development, they turned to the Gallery who provided training in Visual Thinking Strategies, a questioning technique that has become popular with not only art educators but many medical and mental health professionals. Furthermore, this strong partnership resulted in the collaborative development of *Expressions: Creativity in Mental Health*, a one-day free conference held at the National Gallery for mental health professionals and clients in May 2008.

This community consultation has fueled and informed the wide variety of adapted and inclusive programs offered by the National Gallery. In response to the Gallery's national mandate the accessibility educator has offered on-site training to several other museums in Canada on how they too may develop their own accessibility strategy. Based on this national need to create dialogue and training, and building on the success of *Expressions*, the National Gallery organized the first Canadian conference on museum accessibility titled *Connections, Collections and Communities: Making Museums and Galleries in Canada inclusive and accessible* in October 2009. Although the accessibility educator's 3-year term ended in November 2009, the National Gallery continues to regularly offer Art for All programs, including the inclusive program Stimulating the Senses, developed to make art accessible for all visitors.

STIMULATING THE SENSES

It's 6:30 pm on a Thursday evening at the Gallery. A small group of 10 adults, from ages 24 to 75, are sitting silently in a small circle of chairs in the Gallery's Rideau Street Convent Chapel. Sighted participants are seated wearing blindfolds or with their eyes shut, while blind or partially sighted participants sit with their white canes or guide dogs resting on the floor near their feet. They are participating in the inclusive monthly program, Stimulating the Senses.

In teams of two, they cup personal CD players in their laps while listening intently through headsets. Aside from the occasional quick breaths, gasps or short laughs, they sit here in silence for over 12 minutes. Gradually, it becomes obvious through their body language that the track they were listening to has come to an end. Headsets and blindfolds are slowly removed. A Gallery guide asks them about their experience.

"The sound, it was amazing. I've never heard anything like it. You could hear the airplane soar right over head," shares Angelo.[4] Angelo is blind and a regular Stimulating the Senses participant. In fact he has been a regular program participant since he first started coming to the Gallery four years ago with the Canadian Council of the Blind.

Angelo and the other participants have just finished experiencing Janet

Cardiff's Louisiana Walk (1996). Cardiff made a series of audio 'walks' which are audio based artworks recorded in binaural audio to create an exceptionally real sound experience for the listener. She explains:

> The format of the audio walks are similar to that of an audio guide. You are given a CD player or ipod and told to stand or sit in a particular spot and press play. On the CD you hear my voice giving directions, like "turn left here" or "go through this gateway", layered on a background of sounds: the sound of my footsteps, traffic, birds, and miscellaneous sound effects that have been pre-recorded on the same site as they are being heard. This is the important part of the recording. The virtual recorded soundscape has to mimic the real physical one in order to create a new world as a seamless combination of the two. My voice gives directions but also relates thoughts and narrative elements, which instils in the listener a desire to continue and finish the walk.
>
> All of my walks are recorded in binaural audio with multi-layers of sound effects, music, and voices (sometimes as many as 18 tracks) added to the main walking track to create a 3D sphere of sound. Binaural audio is a technique that uses miniature microphones placed in the ears of a person. The result is an incredibly lifelike 3D reproduction of sound. Played back on a headset, it is almost as if the recorded events were taking place live.[5]

Cardiff works in collaboration with George Bures Miller and each experience often feels personal. As Cardiff explains, the walks are designed so that audience members have the opportunity to experience them on location where it was recorded. However for many, such an opportunity is rare and their experience of the walk will be off-site, providing a different understanding of the work. In Stimulating the Senses the context of the artwork is provided and included in the dialogue of the experience.

Following Angelo's lead, participants start to share their experience with the artwork. Some relate the work to personal memories, while others talk about what they visualized in their minds. The discussion is quickly full swing, with people patiently waiting to speak, while others choose to simply listen. The Gallery guide occasionally adds small tidbits of information about the artist, about audio-based art and about a previous audio work by Cardiff—*The Forty Part Motet* (2001)—that had been installed in this very space located in the Canadian galleries. Predominantly however, the program consists of participants—an extremely diverse mix of ages, life experiences and abilities—experiencing and sharing their opinions on art with each other. This is precisely what makes this program accessible: it requires no previous knowledge of art, art history or the artist. It simply requires that you show up and participate.

Stimulating the Senses was developed as an inclusive museum program, designed to bring together visitors with and without visual impairments. It was first piloted in April 2007 and since, hundreds of visitors have attended. The program is offered monthly in both French and English and registration is limited to groups of 12. Spaces are reserved to help ensure an equal mix of both visitors who are blind or partially sighted and visitors without visual impairments. Since starting in 2007 there has been a consistent mix of both repeat and new visitors to the program. The trend seems to be that visitors who are blind or partially sighted come routinely, while there is more turnover from visitors without visual impairments. The program could easily be expanded if the demand exceeded capacity, however at present it meets audience needs. The program typically starts off by introducing participants to each other, the guide and the program theme, followed by a 45-minute multisensory activity in the Gallery and ends with a 25-minute social discussion over tea and coffee.

The concept is simple - to allow visitors the opportunity to share the experience of exploring art using senses other then sight. Multisensory interactive participation and reflective dialogue allows opportunities for participants without previous knowledge of art to participate equally with those who may. Furthermore, participants with visual impairments are able to provide insight and a unique perspective on art, which sighted visitors, may not have been exposed to otherwise; while sighted visitors are able to share perception between what they have experienced and what they see.

As Angelo explains:

> I am not at all bothered by the presence of blind-folded sighted attendees. In fact, I glean insights by hearing their explanations of how their in-the-dark conceptions differ from what they see when they remove their blind-folds.[6]

Likewise a blindfolded sighted visitor shares their experience listening to Cardiff's *Louisiana Walk* (1996):

> That is the first time I thought I knew what it is like to be blind. All the movements coming at me without warnings. I don't think I could handle it without freaking out.[7]

Since its first pilot the program has explored art from many styles and traditions. Participants have touched Marcel Duchamp's *Readymades*, smelled the aromas of a gas station while exploring George Segal's installation *Gas Station* (1963) and listened to storytellers weave tales using imagery from paintings in the collection. One of the first nights included a unique participatory visit by the founder of acoustic ecology and The World Soundscape Project, R. Murray Schafer. Schafer, who travelled from his home in northern Ontario, brought a bag of fresh Ontario apples for participants to bite into, reminding them to take note of the taste, the smell and the sound of this extraordinary and multisensory experience.

More and more gallery visitors are not only looking for new ways to engage with the museum and art, but with each other. The more opportunities they are given to have interactive experiences and to tap into multiple senses the more likely they are to learn and remember their experience. As Richard Sandell points out "The data suggests that heightened levels of audience activity mean that audiences are indeed likely to 'notice', attend to and engage with the museum."[8]

CAUGHT IN THE ACT: PARTICIPATORY ART AND ITS POTENTIAL FOR INCLUSIVE MUSEUMS EXPERIENCES

So if visitors have more meaningful experiences and learn more when they are actively engaged through multiple senses, the next question one might ask is, how? The PLEASE DO NOT TOUCH THE ARTWORK warning is in place to preserve and protect collections from damage, so that they may be available for future generations. One of the challenges for museum educators then, is making seemingly non-interactive artworks such as paintings, interactive. For example touching a painting is not only relatively uninformative, but also usually impossible due to the damage that would cause. Facilitating experiences that are interactive or multi-modal may include touch but it is important to remember that it is but one sense and approach. Instead of touching a painting, museum educators may describe the artwork using verbal description to help participants create mental images as well as employ didactic elements such as storytelling, music, or offering touchable non-art objects to help convey an understanding of the work. These teaching methods are in a way a type of translation or interpretation, which are helpful in creating greater access to a wider variety of artworks. However, as with any language, the more levels of translation and interpretation that occur, the farther away we stem from the actual meaning trying to be conveyed. Thus the more interaction that can occur with the original artwork, the closer we get to the actual meaning and the greater the understanding. If the original artwork is created with the intention of interaction as with participatory art, the opportunity for learning is potentially at its highest.

In 2008, the National Gallery of Canada mounted the exhibition Caught in the Act: The Viewer as Performer, which at the time was the largest contemporary art exhibition the Gallery had hosted in over 10 years. The exhibition explored the history of participatory art in Canada and the role of the viewer as an active component of these artworks. In her introduction to *Caught in the Act: Viewer as Performer* (exhibition catalog), curator Josée Drouin-Brisebois writes,

> Developing out of histories of performance, installation, environmental, minimal and body art, the works in the exhibition foreground the interaction between art object and viewing subject and consider the conventional relationship between the work, the artist and the spectator.[9]

This exhibition happened to run during the weeklong Masters Series Workshop for adults who are blind or partially sighted, held at the National Gallery during White Cane Week in February 2009. White Cane Week as a national awareness campaign organized by the Canadian Council of the Blind to promote public awareness about the lives and experiences of blind or partially sighted Canadians.[10] Masters Series Workshops are a series of specially designed half-day studio workshops, allowing participants to immerse themselves in a topic or theme, while becoming acquainted with the Gallery, its staff and the collection. They are developed in collaboration with various community groups and designed to meet the specific needs and interests of the group. The workshops are hands-on, seeking to develop both art-making skills and art literacy, often with groups who might not of received appropriate or adapted art education from mainstream studio programs. The series is also offered for free and the Gallery makes every attempt to accommodate transportation and interpretation requests.

Caught in the Act provided several opportunities for participants to have multisensory interactions with artwork, and thus, gain a better understanding of the exhibition. "The show is rooted in the anthropological premise that we learn more from experience with works of art then from their interpretation"[11] explains Drouin-Brisebois. Although participants explored the work of several artists in the exhibition, including Kent Monkman's *Boudoir de Berdashe* (2007) and BGL's *The Discourse of Elements* (2006), the art work that the workshop series focused most heavily upon, was Massimo Guerrera's *A Hypen Between The Visible and The Invisible (Darboral)* (2000-2008). This installation took over an entire room in the exhibition, from the multi-textured coverings on the floor to the web of white and copper wires strung across the room from the ceiling. *Darboral* was not only filled with various sculptural objects made by the artist, but also the living artefacts left from experiences that had taken place in the space over the 8 years of its transformative existence. This included hair left by visitors, crates and packing foam, notes with the written names of people who had come to the space, scraps of eaten vegetables and fruits, and plants that had grown from the seeds.[12] Soft, inviting places to sit, surrounded the space and when visitors entered *Darboral* they were invited to remove their shoes and experience. Guerrera explains: "In the end, *Darboral* platform exists only in the present moment of the experience, it is a continuum in constant transformation [that] pursues its organic process in the minds of those who experience it"[13]

Participants in the Master Series Workshop entered Guerrera's *Darboral* several times and having been given 'carte blanche' of what they could touch, were allotted an opportunity to have a more thorough understanding of the space. This interaction with various sensory elements in the installation were later used as inspiration for their own personal creations including sculptural based works using plaster and found objects.

Darboral is not only the space itself, but everything that happens in the space.[14] Because of the importance the artist places on the experience of personal interaction[15], Massimo Guerrera visited the gallery space on several occasions throughout the exhibition to interact with visitors. The last of these visits coincided with the White Cane Week Master Series Workshops, allowing participants and the artist to exchange an intimate and personal dialogue. Afterwards, both the artist and the participants expressed having a memorable and meaningful experience that held personal significance to them.

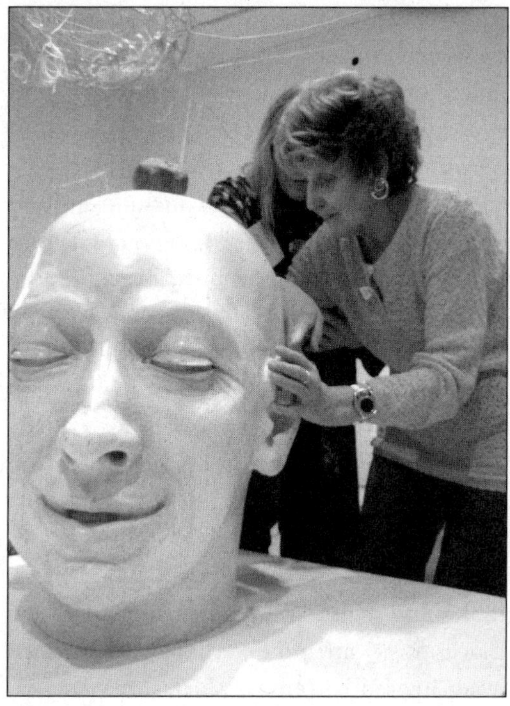

Theresa, a blind visitor, touches a sculpture in the exhibition Caught in the Act at National Gallery of Canada. Massimo Guerrera, *A Hypen Between the Visible and the Invisible (Darboral), 2000–2008*. Mixed media installation, installation dimensions variable National Gallery of Canada, Ottawa © Massimo Guerrera, courtesy Clint Roenisch. *Photo © NGC.*

I didn't like the installation the first time I went in. I felt frustrated with all the getting up and down and the objects everywhere that Erie [guide dog] could get into. There was so much going on and I didn't know what I was touching; it was confusing. But when I met with Massimo, and we sat and talked about just a couple objects, it made a big difference. It was a really moving experience. Now it is one of my favourite artworks. I already have ideas of things I want to make at home! —Christine, Master Series Workshop Participant/ Artist [16]

This is an example of where participatory art has provided a participant with a meaningful and memorable experience which transformed her opinion about a particular artwork, and later also inspired her in her own artistic practice. These are outcomes that gallery educators often aspire to in the development of educational programs for the general public. It is important to also note that visitors who are blind or partially sighted, at least those in Canada, have witnessed a long history of limited (if not non-existent) access to travelling or special exhibitions, due to the inability to acquire permission for touching access from lending institutions, and/or the unwillingness of museums and galleries to seek out permission from conservators. Caught in the Act and the support of both the education and curatorial departments provided new and meaningful opportunities for visitors who were not granted access to special exhibitions in the past.

THE VISITOR EXPERIENCE: GETTING OUT OF *GETTING IT RIGHT*

It is also important to note Christine's frustration with being confused and uncomfortable while first encountering participatory art. Certainly she is not alone in this response. How often have we as museum educators heard a visitor's confused cry of "I don't get it", while trying to decipher the invitation to interact with contemporary art? One could speculate that the need for the "right answer" is heightened by the need to conceive of an appropriate physical response, which is far more extroverted, then when simply walking by, hiding any potential confusion internally. However it is the very action of getting out of our routine and entering into a space of confusion that creates meaningful experiences, and thus art. As Ann-Marie Ninacs explains, in reference to Guerrera's *Darboral* "Our propensity to hang on to our habits, to avoid risk, and to seek success at all costs is an unconscious attempt to escape death, which has at the very unfortunate effect of separating us from life. Therefore, by participating *in a work*, that takes us along an unknown path, we fundamentally contribute *to creation*."[17]

Even within the participatory program Stimulating the Senses, which aims to create a welcoming space for participants to experiment with new modes of experience, several sighted participants have voiced a similar feeling of discomfort by all of a sudden switching off their dominant sense of sight, and having to rely on their less developed senses. As one participant reflected after her first time participating in Stimulating the Senses, "being suddenly sightless is highly disconcerting. I know, it's obvious. But I don't think you get it until it's gone. I didn't, at any rate."[18]

She then goes on to say:

As the guide was describing the art, I kept adding more to the picture in my head. White wooden window frame here, cans stacked there, oh, glass in the window frames, this stark white figure here, that colour black the background. As she talked, I felt a growing frustration—growing towards anxiety—that what was in my head wasn't *right*. I desperately wanted to take the blindfold off. I noticed that I did and let it go. Just my body's reaction to having its normal touch points removed so quickly. Anything that helps me give up on needing to Get It Right is something I should do more often.[19]

As this visitor points out, just because an experience might be challenging or uncomfortable, is not an excuse to avoid it. Typically sighted participants in Stimulating the Senses often report a similar experience– that the experience was new, challenging and at times difficult and even scary. What is most important here, is that almost all of the time, it was observed that the same participants reported being thankful for the opportunity. This leads to the suggestion that visitors are looking for precisely those kinds of challenges and opportunities to engage with art, in ways they have never tried before, even if it's hard. Does art not in some capacity aim to challenge us, challenge what we think we know or feel? This in turn, often requires us to also reflect. This reflection is perhaps not easy, but a necessary element of personal development. Guerrera seems fully aware of the situation he places the visitor as Ninacs observes, "This journey *is not easy*. Letting go of what we know and committing oneself to exposing who we truly are is always an unsettling exercise; even when there is no audience but oneself."[20]

CONCLUSION

If we wish to diversify our audiences in a meaningful way and truly open up our doors to people who do not typically feel welcome, museums must fuel what Josée Drouin-Brisebois refers to as the "latent potential of the gallery as a site for social engagement".[21] We do this by developing programs in constant consultation with the very people we wish to reach and develop exhibitions that provide new opportunities for engagement. To diversify our audiences we must diversify our organizations, our staff and our exhibitions. We must expand how we see citizenship and whom we view as cultural contributors. To tap into these diverse perspectives we must start employing and consulting Deaf and disabled scholars, historians and artists and start examining the authentic representation of Deaf and disability culture in the collections of museums and galleries. Deaf and disabled visitors are more likely to want to visit a museum and participate in programming, if they are provided meaningful ways to access collections and most importantly see their art, their history, their language and authentic reflections of themselves, represented in exhibitions. Museums need to be rooted in a desire to bring visitors together through their shared human experiences, as well as facilitate opportunities for the expression of their diverse perspectives.

To touch, to interact, to share, are all personal experiences. Like in Stimulating the Senses, where the program is based on visitors' memories and personal multisensory experiences, participatory art also relies on the visitor to get out of their conventional gallery visiting routine and allow an opportunity to open up to the unknown. It is precisely this participation and this opportunity for personal perspective and experience, which allows for new entry points of access and thus potential for new audiences. Each person has a different experience and response to a new situation. To have this response does not require a certain skill set or art historical expertise. It does not even require that you can see the art. What is required is providing an opportunity for both social and multisensory engagement on the part of the museum and a willingness to participate on the part of the visitor.

Notes

1. Penny Leclair during Stimulating the Senses, April 2007, National Gallery of Canada, Ottawa.
2. Benjamin Fredembach, Anne Hillairet de Boisferon, Edouard Gentaz, "Learning of Arbitrary Association between Visual and Auditory Novel Stimuli in Adults: The 'Bond Effect' of Haptic Exploration," *PLoS ONE* (Public Library of Science), Vol. 4, Issue 3, (2009), http://dx.doi.org/10.1371%2Fjournal.pone.0004844
3. Ladan Shams, Aaron R. Seitz, "Benefits of multisensory learning," *Trends in Cognitive Sciences*, 1 November 2008, Vol. 12, Issue 11, 411–417, http://linkinghub.elsevier.com/retrieve/pii/S1364661308002180
4. Angelo DeMarsico during Stimulating the Senses, March 26, 2009, National Gallery of Canada, Ottawa.
5. Janet Cardiff, "Introduction to the Audio Walks," posted on the artist's website, Janet Cardiff George Bures Miller, http://www.cardiffmiller.com/artworks/walks/index.html#
6. Angelo DeMarsico, e-mail message to author, July 15, 2009.
7. Participant during Stimulating the Senses, March 26, 2009, National Gallery of Canada, Ottawa.
8. Richard Sandell, *Museums, Prejudice and the Reframing of Difference*, (Oxon: Routledge, 2007), 109.
9. Josée Drouin-Brisebois, "Close Encounters," in *Caught in the Act: The Viewer as Performer*, an exhibition catalog, curated by Josée Drouin-Brisebois. (Ottawa: National Gallery of Canada, 2008), 25–26.
10. Canadian Council of the Blind, "White Cane Week History," http://www.ccbnational.net/new/index.php?White_Cane_Week
11. Drouin-Brisebois, 70.
12. Anne-Marie Ninacs, "Exercises in Living", in *Caught in the Act: The Viewer as Performer*, an exhibition catalog, curated by Josée Drouin-Brisebois. (Ottawa: National Gallery of Canada, 2008), 206.

13. Massimo Guerrera, "Darboral. Un trait d'union entre le Visible at l'invisible." Text of a lecture given at Oboro, Montreal, April 8, 2008, 4; quotation modified by author (Ninacs), quoted in Ninacs, 206.
14. Ninacs, 206.
15. Drouin-Brisebois, 62.
16. Christine, in conversation with author, February 5, 2009, National Gallery of Canada, Ottawa.
17. Ninacs, 212.
18. Megan Butcher, blog entry titled "Stimulated" posted on Radial Symmetry, posted February 26, 2009, http://meganbutcher.com/blog/Stimulated. (Accessed August 7, 2009).
19. Ibid.
20. Ninacs, 211.
21. Drouin-Brisebois, 62.

References

Drouin-Brisebois, Josée (Curator), Greg A Hill, Stephen Horne and Anne-Marie Ninacs. 2008. *Caught in the Act: The Viewer as Performer,* Ottawa: National Gallery of Canada. This catalogue accompanies the exhibition "Caught in the Act: The Viewer as Performer" organized by the National Gallery of Canada and presented in Ottawa from 17 October 2008 to 15 February 2009

Fredembach, Benjamin, Anne Hillairet de Boisferon, Edouard Gentaz. 2009. Learning of Arbitrary Association between Visual and Auditory Novel Stimuli in Adults: The "Bond Effect" of Haptic Exploration. *PLoS ONE (Public Library of Science)* Vol. 4, Issue 3, (March 16, 2009) http://dx.doi.org/10.1371%2Fjournal.pone.0004844 (accessed August 3, 2009)

Sandell, Richard. 2007. *Museums, Prejudice and the Reframing of Difference,* Oxon: Routledge.

Shams, Ladan, Aaron R. Seitz. 2008. Benefits of multisensory learning. *Trends in Cognitive Sciences,* no.1 Vol. 12, Issue 11, 411-417 (November 2008) http://linkinghub.elsevier.com/retrieve/pii/S1364661308002180

Elizabeth Sweeney was the accessibility educator at the National Gallery of Canada from 2006 to 2009. She developed and expanded the Art for All accessibility programs and organized the first Canadian conference on museum accessibility titled Connections, Collections and Communities. She received a BFA from Concordia University and a B.Ed from the University of Ottawa. She is currently working towards a Masters of Critical Disability Studies at York University. Her area of research is on the representation of disability culture in Canadian museums.

Mixed Identity
The Invisible Majority

Nancy Arms Simon

Abstract   Although cultures have blended in the Americas for over 500 years, people who do not consider themselves "mixed" still require cross-cultural precedents to identify the threads of their lineage. The absence of "mixed" as an option in our forms, culture, and thinking creates a skewed identity crisis for people of multiple backgrounds. As globalization brings our world closer together every day, it is imperative that we try to see others as they would choose to be seen, or we are interacting with an inaccurate picture.

We used to think that when we have completed our study of one, we knew two, because "two" is "one" and "one." We are finding that we still must make a study of "and."

Sir Arthur Eddington (1882–1944)

People who are of mixed gender, transgender, transsexual, or gender-fluid have much in common with people of mixed cultural backgrounds. Primarily, both groups understand the self-awareness needed to create an identity when one is not clearly bestowed upon them. Unlike either of two parts, a person of mixed identity must cultivate a third, positive identity, and often, has to defend that identity to a world that would have everything in black in white.

In my two-year study of contemporary art and writings, I have found that few people are able to make this leap of consciousness. Fewer still are the artists that are creating work about their solutions to this dilemma. The artists whose work is available for exhibition agreed to participate in the exhibit *Mixed: The Study of "And."*

Journal of Museum Education, Volume 34, Number 3, Fall 2009, pp. 249–254.

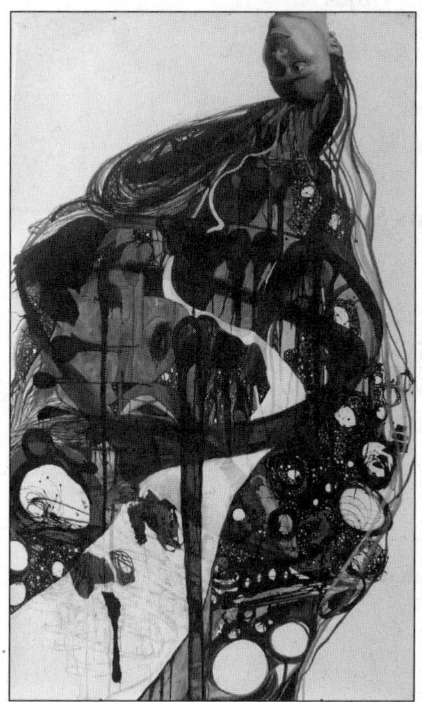

Left, Mequitta Ahuja, *Insemination,* 84" × 52", enamel on paper, 2007; right, Mequitta Ahuja, *Off the Edge,* oil on canvas, 96" × 72", 2008; opposite page, Mequitta Ahuja, *Spark,* waxy chalk on paper, 50" × 114", 2009.

Currently searching for an appropriate venue, it is the curator's hope that this exhibit will foster discussion about our collective views on mixed identity and ideally, provide an outline on which people of mixed identity can model their own identity resolutions. The exhibit may also serve as an example of how to bring complicated conversations about LGBTQ and cultural diversity into gallery and museum contexts.

When museums and galleries consider how to develop programming, collections, and outreach strategies aimed at diversifying their audiences to include LGBTQ people, museums can use the research that has been done on race-based thinking as a model. As a result of my interest in identity and how artists explore this concept in their work, I created an exhibit that deals with the complexity of identity entitled *Mixed: The Study of "And."* The participating artists, all of mixed heritage, have created work about their experience. I am interested in how exhibits like *Mixed: The Study of "And"* can help museums work towards LGTBQ diversity.

One of the first things for museums to consider is whether they are

trying to engage with the entire LGBTQ community or just one part of it. With *Mixed: The Study of "And,"* for example, I hope to attract transgendered people. I do not expect that the issues will be relevant to all members of the LGTBQ community Once research has been done to find out what specific communities the museum hopes to engage with, museum staff can approach specific community members to seek potential collaborators. Thoughtful research into the language, issues and cultural references will help facilitate initial conversations.

The courtship of any historically silenced group is more successful when it is somewhat organic. With LGTBQ individuals, everyone has unique experience. For example, people may have very different experiences of coming out, relationships with family members, etc.

The most effective way to create a long-term relationship with a target community is to engage a group of community advisors and work with them in an open and transparent way The aim of this partnership is to create lasting relationships, sustainable programs, and avoid the pitfalls of one-off events. Tokenistic programming can lead to unrealistically raised expectations and ultimately do more harm than good. To create meaningful and responsive programming across the institution, the community advisory can work with staff and volunteers to generate successful community engagement. Being open to constructive criticism and conducting program evaluation go a long way to "queering" the museum.

When developing collections or planning exhibitions, bringing in artists who can critically engage with the existing collection is a creative way to reinterpretation through another lens. For example, artists like Fred Wilson and James Luna use provocative interventions to effectively deal with previously absent histories from collections.

Nathan Gibbs, *Race Cube,* 2003.

An internal assessment of staff, board, and volunteers is an important step to ensure that LGBTQ people are represented in the institution. The development of a training module and specific policies will help to facilitate an environment that is knowledgeable about and welcoming to these communities. Hiring staff at all levels, including decision-making positions, will help to ensure systemic change. For LGTBQ staff, working in a museum during a transitional time can require patience, humor, and generosity of spirit as the museum evolves towards equity. For example, for transgendered staff, being referred to using the wrong gendered pronoun will be trying. There will be challenges, and the change process can be unnecessarily messy.

Since the 1960s, shifts in race-based thinking have resulted in a proliferation of writing and art-making about mixed racial identities. The federal government, did not recognize these shifts in thinking and "Mixed" was only added as an option for the U.S. in 2000. Adults who completed the census prior to 2000 were forced to identify falsely.

When I started working on *Mixed: The Study of "And,"* I wanted to include the work of transgendered artists and artists of mixed cultural heritage. There are common experiences among people whose identities straddle categories of ethnicity, sexuality, gender, and so forth. In a society bent on categorization, people in these communities often find themselves explaining their identity.

The exhibit will show the common experiences of people of mixed heritages regardless of how they have been racialized or gendered. The chosen work stretches over a broad range of topics, from the very literal (e.g., Mike Tauber) to that in need of deeper artistic interpretation (Mequitta Ahuja) to the thoughtful punch line (Nathan Gibbs). The exhibit can challenge audiences about the process of creating identity.

I see *Mixed: The Study of And* as appealing to a broad section of the public, because in today's globalized world, many people have experienced being part of more than one community. Being relevant and responsive to ways in which notions of identity are constantly changing will go along way to helping museums engage a broad public.

Nancy Arms Simon *works at the Labor Archives and Research Center at San Francisco State University as Archive Registrar. She is currently finishing her Master's thesis in Museum Studies at S.F. State, an exhibit called* Occupation: Economic Justice As A Civil Right In San Francisco 1963–64 *slated for February 2010 at the San Francisco Public Library. Born and raised between the Wisconsin countryside and the liberal island of Madison, (WI) Nancy moved to San Francisco in 1998, and feels that she makes a kind of sense here. She lives with her husband and son, and enjoys hearing multiple languages on the walk to the grocery store as well as seeing the variety of skin colors on the SF State campus. Nancy's ancestors are of German, Scottish, African-American, and Cherokee Indian stock. She is desperately seeking an appropriate venue for her exhibit* Mixed: The Study of "And."

From the Margins to the Core
Aims, Outcomes, and Legacies of the Capacity Building and Cultural Ownership Project

Eithne Nightingale

Abstract   The article explores lessons learned from the Victoria and Albert (V&A) Museum's Capacity Building and Cultural Ownership Project — working with culturally diverse communities, a three-year, one-million pound project funded by the Heritage Lottery Fund from 2005–2008. The project had several aims. To research and develop the V&A's collections in relation to culturally diverse communities;1 to increase the percentages of BAME (black, Asian, and minority ethnic) audiences and contribute to intercultural understanding and social cohesion; to develop effective partnerships between the museum and black and ethnic minority organizations and to leave a lasting legacy both within the V&A and the sector as a whole. Drawing on external evaluation, this article reviews what was and was not achieved, indicating directions for the future in order to ensure long-term and lasting change.

In 2005, the V&A embarked on an ambitious £978,000 three-year Heritage Lottery Fund funded (HLF) program focusing on cultural diversity. It was a cross-departmental initiative and involved all three sites of the Museum — the V&A at South Kensington, the Museum of Childhood in Bethnal Green, and the Theater Museum in Covent Garden. The project built on earlier work by the V&A, including a previous smaller-scale HLF-funded program from 2000–2002.

There were three strands to the program.[2] Strand 1, "Hidden Histories," related to the museum's collections. Objectives included uncovering and exploring the hidden histories of the museum collections (in particular those of relevance to the African Diaspora) and their connections with contem-

Journal of Museum Education, Volume 34, Number 3, Fall 2009, pp. 255–270.

Conference on Fashioning Diasporas, V&A May 2009. Percentage of overall audiences from black and ethnic minority backgrounds has increased from 8% in 2001/2 to 15% in 2008/9. 8–9 % of UK population is from a BAME background.

porary cultures and faiths. It also sought to develop new collections which reflected the diverse backgrounds of London's communities, in particular, Black and Asian UK theater over the past 50 years (Theater Collections), and childhood in the East End of London (Museum of Childhood).

Strand 2, "Access, Learning, Social Inclusion, and Cohesion," focused on audiences. Key objectives included attracting a more diverse audience to the museum and increasing intercultural and interfaith understanding, thus contributing to social inclusion and cohesion. These objectives were to be achieved through a range of public programs, learning opportunities, and resources based on previous research, taking into account the needs of diverse visitors.

Strand 3, "Partnerships, Capacity Building, and Cultural Ownership," was largely concerned with building capacity in both BAME organizations and the V&A in the area of heritage and cultural diversity. It sought to develop mutually beneficial partnerships and to provide training in heritage skills according to individual and organizational need. The project also aimed to open up opportunities for people from diverse backgrounds to work in museums as volunteers, on work placements, or as paid employees. The final overarching objective was to contribute to a change in V&A policies and practices over the longer term.

There were a range of questions that were to be addressed in the final evaluation. Strand 1 questions focused on whether the project increased knowledge of the African objects and colonial/post colonial attitudes to collecting, or of the links between V&A historical collections and contemporary cultures and faiths. Other questions were specific to the Museum of Childhood and the Theater Collections. For example, did the project demonstrate the importance of the collection of tangible and intangible heritage by and from people of diverse backgrounds to making such collections more representative of multiracial Britain?

Strand 2 questions focused on whether related programs were successful in bringing in more culturally diverse audiences, and groups from lower socioeconomic backgrounds. There were further, more qualitative questions. Did the project increase the pride of people in their own heritage? Did it encourage exploration of differences and commonalities between cultures? Last, did the Project have an impact on the overall profile of V&A visitors?

Strand 3 questions were perhaps the most challenging. Did the project strengthen the capacity of organizations outside the V&A to research and explore their own heritage? Did it strengthen partnerships between the V&A and BAME organizations, to provide training, work experience, and volunteer opportunities; and did it encourage effective interdepartmental and interagency work? And finally, was the project successful in contributing to long-term change at the V&A and having an impact on the heritage sector as a whole?[3]

The focus of much of the project evaluation was summative using focus groups, interviews, meta-analysis, opinion polling, qualitative research, questionnaires, and structured interviewing. Under formative evaluation, a social network analysis was carried out which focused on relationships within the organization and identification of key partnerships.

Eight staff people were employed on the Project, although only Machel Bogues, the Project Manager, was full time. Others worked three to four days a week. This included Helen Mears, the African Research Fellow; Janet Browne, Audience Development Officer (African Caribbean); Marilyn Greene, Intercultural/Interfaith Officer; Julie Begum, World in the East End Coordinator; Denise Drake, Web Manager; Margot Rodway-Brown, Capacity Building and Training Officer; and Rosie Cooper, Project Administrator. The salaries were the highest cost against the project. Other cost elements were public programs, the Web, training, networking events, etc.

That the project was ambitious is not in doubt and particularly in such a large, complex organization as the V&A. The project ended officially in September 2008 and there are clear signs of what the project achieved and its actual and potential legacy. There are also indications of the challenges the project experienced.

The most significant legacy relates to the V&A's position on its African collections. Senior managers remarked,

> Using a research fellow on the collections, particularly Africa, placed in the Research Department, was a good idea and allowed focus.[4]

And again,

> Recognizing the African collections in the museum is the biggest legacy of the project.[5]

The significance of this change may not be appreciated unless the history of collecting at the V&A is better understood. The V&A collecting policy defines the geographical boundaries for collecting as follows,

> Objects are collected from all major artistic traditions of Europe and Asia. The Museum does not normally collect pre-European settlement material from the Americas and Australasia. The Museum does not collect historic material from Oceania and Africa south of the Sahara."[6]

As Helen Mears, the African Research Fellow, writes,

> The idea that, simply, "the V&A does not collect African art" is prevalent and is presented as fact by Museum visitors, front-of-house staff, even curators, who have all been heard stating the 'fact' that the V&A does not hold African material in its permanent collections.[7]

Yet in 2003–2004 curators identified a significant body of material that had some connection to Africa or the African Diaspora. As research (2005–2008) progressed, at least 4300 items of African material were identified. However, few of the objects had public access descriptions or photographs and sometimes there was little more than basic documentary descriptions.[8]

More recently acquired work by contemporary African artists and Black British artists in "Word and Image," the only department to be pro-active in this area, were better documented. [9]

The research carried out under this program has clearly established that African art and design has always been an important element of the V&A's collections. Some objects were purchased through the Great Exhibition and North African material was collected throughout the nineteenth and early twentieth centuries. Other objects, including some from Ghana, were acquired through Britain's imperial activities, and later through the Circulation Department.

Helen Mears, the African Research Fellow, points out that while some may argue the V&A risks duplication, notably with the Museum of London or the British Museum, no other London museum specializes in the study of decorative arts and design history, and that it is inappropriate to tell a global history of art and design without acknowledging the contribution of African art and production.

Furthermore the V&A's Access, Inclusion, and Diversity Strategy makes clear the aspiration that the collections should not only inspire and broaden people's experience in relation to art, design, and craftsmanship but also relate to people's cultural heritage.[10]A premise of the project was that the African Caribbean community in the UK is too significant a presence not to be represented within the V&A collections, nor can European art be understood without reference to the influence of African art, for example, on the Surrealists or Picasso.

Such a change in V&A policy and practice, a legacy itself of colonial attitudes where art from sub-Saharan Africa was classified as anthropology and therefore considered the remit of the British Museum, opens the way to reassessing the V&A's focus on Asia and Europe.

As another senior colleague states,

A more systematic collection of non-European and the Americas is needed. [11]

The Museum has responded positively to the findings of the research, setting up an African collections group, mainly, but not exclusively of curators.

The discovery of the African objects enabled curators to look at the collection from a Black heritage point of view and, as a result, the collections group has been formed.[12]

In the absence of an African gallery, the work of the African Research Fellow has been invaluable as the inspiration for a range of Black heritage programs organized by the African Caribbean Development Officer.

"Helen was my gallery," Janet Browne, the Audience Development Officer (African Caribbean) explained.[13]

The research was particularly valuable in the development of gallery trails and public programs related to slavery, alongside the V&A contemporary exhibition, Uncomfortable Truths to mark the two-hundredth anniversary of the parliamentary abolition of slavery in 2007.[14] Participants were impressed with the museum's attempt to acknowledge Black heritage,

Having a Black culture event at the V&A increased my pride as I feel we are getting a sense of recognition.[15]

Of the respondents attending Black heritage workshops, all believed the events had increased their knowledge of the African museum collections. In particular, they picked up on the links with Africa and the slave trade, and how it helped demonstrate how the slave trade contributed so much to the development of the UK. But another participant thought the museum was showing

a white-washed history, especially regarding the slave trade.[16]

This participant felt that the labeling of the exhibits was not detailed enough and therefore,

de-contextualized a lot of things.[17]

One participant appreciated the museum's attempt to diversify activities but wondered whether

it may just be doing it to tick a box.[18]

Another remarked that the African collection wasn't on a par with other collections. This was seen as

a missed opportunity, and may put people off. [19]

The event left her confused, as she felt it was meant to encourage visitors from a Black heritage but did not have a gallery dedicated to African collections. Another respondent pointed out there were not enough collections in relation to Caribbean History. The participant argued that with such a large population of people with Caribbean roots in the UK, the museum would benefit from extending this area of the collection.

Given the lack of objects from the Africa or the Caribbean on display, the Audience Development Officer (African Caribbean) was endlessly inventive in developing events related to the V&A public program. In addition, she was able to use her extensive networks within the Black community to inform her event planning and to source relevant artists. In 2006, she worked with the Families Team in developing a Cuba Afrique festival alongside the Che Guevara exhibiton. The 60s fashion display inspired programs focusing on Black style and culture of the period, including a very successful evening organised jointly with Laura Elliot, Social Inclusion Officer, where ska, blue beat, and reggae enthusiasts mixed with fans of Northern Soul. Sometimes the connection with the exhibition was tenuous. It would be much better if considerations of diversity were automatically incorporated into the initial planning of any exhibition. In fact, partly attributable to the project, considering diversity at initial inception is now the agreed-upon practice in the museum-wide revised exhibition guidelines. Clearly such embedding of diversity into initial planning has a long-term potential impact given the draw of temporary exhibitions in bringing in new, diverse visitors.

The lessons for the future are apparent. More has to be done to ensure that the objects related to Africa and the African Diaspora achieve higher visibility through galleries, displays, web site, publications, exhibitions, and other public programs. Care needs to be taken to ensure events are not perceived as token and to take account of sensitivities of communities who have previously felt marginalized. Programs need to be ambitious and large-scale, such as the Motown weekend, that attracted visitors from all backgrounds and developed alongside the "Story of the Supremes" exhibition. Others, such as the work with young black boys from Eastside Young Leaders Academy, or with mental health users, need to be smaller in scale and more targeted. Such programs need support from the Museum as a whole, including through effective marketing. We will be able to have a significant impact on overall visitor figures only by a more sustained audience development approach that does not rely on one-off programs or ignore the diverse interests and aspirations of Black and other audiences.

The work of the Intercultural and Interfaith Development Officer, Marilyn Greene, straddled strands 1 and 2. Initially she worked with curators in identifying collections of relevance to diverse cultures. Members of seven faith advisory groups—Sikh, Hindu, Buddhist, Islam, Christian, Jain, and Jewish—selected objects of particular significance. They supplied additional information, commented on outdated terminology, contributed ideas on interpretation, exhibitions, and public programs.

Initially, members of the project team were keen that such contributions be added to the V&A official documentation as under the Museums Library and Archives (MLA) Revisiting Collections initiative. There was resistance internally, these records being regarded as the responsibility of curators. A compromise was reached by integrating 'community responses' into the relevant collections part of the website.[20] Towards the end of the project however the Intercultural and Interfaith Development Officer brought all of the groups responses together into a final report. This was presented and circulated to people across the Museum. Curators cross-checked the information and revised and added the advisory groups suggestions to the V&A official documentation where appropriate. In retrospect it is surprising that we did not come to this solution earlier. Perhaps, it was the growing recognition of the project's work that created a more receptive climate to community perspectives once the information had found to be valid. After all many members of the advisory groups were themselves academics or experts in their field.

The changing position of Judaica in the Museum is an interesting point. Ten years ago the Judaica silver collection of the V&A was housed in several cases within the Church Plate gallery, its name masking the fact that it also housed Judaica. Now it sits clearly marked within a stunning renamed Sacred Silver and Stained Glass Gallery opened in 2005.

The metalwork curator responded positively to the advisory group's wish that the Museum continues to collect both old and contemporary Judaica and outlined various positive developments in this area. There is a display of Judaica (3 objects) from the Gilbert Collection in the Sacred Silver and Stained Glass Galleries (Oct 2009—Oct 2010), for example, and Judaica

Models from the Arab fashion show held in the Madejski gardens at the V&A during the Arab week-end to launch the opening of the Jameel gallery of Middle Eastern Islamic art 2006.

objects from the Gilbert collection may, in the future, tour Jewish museums internationally .These changes have been achieved through the active interest of key curators and their willingness to seek out and listen to views of members of both the Jewish and Christian communities.

Perhaps partly due to the project, many curators have a growing understanding of the significance of our collections to diverse faith communities. Whilst internally curators are primarily concerned with the collections from an art and design perspective the importance of collections from a faith or cultural perspective for audiences from diverse backgrounds should not be underestimated.

Other aspects of the Intercultural Program included the training of 9 intercultural guides from 7 different faiths and the development of intercultural/interfaith tours targeted at youth and community/faith groups. This was also a suggestion of one of the advisory groups although plans for this program had already started by the time the advisory groups met. Large scale festivals were organised to coincide with the opening of the Sacred Silver and Stained Glass Gallery (2005) and the Jameel Gallery of Middle Eastern Islamic Art (2006). There was a season of winter festivals, a Festival of Light[21] and a Peace and Environment weekend. All programs attracted a higher percentage of

BAME audiences than the general V&A profile, but what was noticeable was that faith or culture specific festivals were often more successful in attracting BAME audiences than ones which tried to bring cultures together, and therefore the specific link between a person's culture and the program may not have been so apparent. A model which seemed to partly resolve this was the series of Jameel week-ends (Persian, Turkish, Arab) and the winter festivals (e.g., Hanukkah, Diwali, Christmas). Both these initiatives, advertised as a group, were successful in attracting a range of BAME audiences, white/mixed/black and Christian/Muslim audiences to Diwali for example. Evaluations confirmed the importance given by some parents from all backgrounds of educating their children about different cultures to their own. For others the motivation was passing on their culture to their children or grandchildren, fearing that it might otherwise be lost.[22]

Of the various questions answered by telephone respondents carried out in 2008, 70 percent said the events had increased their understanding of the commonalities and connections between cultures. Those who replied negatively explained that the event only focused on one faith or culture, or that they already had a good understanding of the basis for the event. Many of the telephone interviewees felt that it was through special events that the V&A's collections were truly revealed. As a result, they felt that they gained a deeper understanding both of the V&A's collections as well as their own culture. They

> gave a sense that the V&A is trying to incorporate different cultures and diversity.[23]

They were also impressed that their cultures had been recognised publicly at an institution. One participant commented that it made them proud that the V&A had held such an event dedicated to their Jewish faith and that it is,

> . . . important and impressive that a museum like the V&A have a collection on it. It's fantastic![24]

One article is far too short to do justice to the Capacity Building and Cultural Ownership Program so I have focused on those aspects identified in the evaluation as most successful, i.e., research into collections and events. However because of initial problems with the evaluation and the scale and the breadth of the project, the evaluation has not touched on some of the less heralded successes. At the Museum of Childhood, researchers from diverse communities were trained and employed as collectors of tangible and intangible heritages for the "World in the East End" project managed by Julie Begum. The results of this research can be accessed through the web site or in the family section of the galleries.[25] The Theater Museum now has five recordings of Black and Asian theater alongside interviews of actors, directors and the public carried out by over 50 mainly BAME participants who signed up for the

East End mixed race family interviewed for the World in the East End project. Their life story is now represented in the Family Gallery at the Museum of Childhood in Bethnal Green.

training courses. This material is on the web,[26] has been integrated into a touring exhibition, and is a valuable source material for the new theater galleries at South Kensington. Further research needs be carried out on the impact on visitors of the display of both intangible and tangible material collected from and by diverse communities and how this enhances the standing of a museum or collections particularly with diverse audiences.

The third strand is another hidden pearl. Over 200 people and 54 organizations ranging from the Zimbabwe Women's Association to the Institute of Race Relations participated in training courses on documentation, conservation, handling objects, oral history, fund raising, partnership, etc. Two successful networking events were run—one about partnership with the GLA and MLA, another about cultural leadership for BAME individuals. In the third year, Margot Rodway-Brown, the Capacity Building and Training Officer, focused on two initiatives. The first was a series of action learning sessions with Elevate, a black-led network of cultural and creative organizations in Brixton; the second a seminar for senior people in the cultural and heritage professions on the business case for diversity.

This was a challenging area of work. As Machel Bogues, the Project Manager, stated:

> Skill sharing rather than capacity building has taken place. Capacity building is problematic because it takes time and training inter-

ventions require a high level of technical knowledge to engage with museum departments.[27]

After all, conservators take years to learn their profession! There is also no specific evaluation of the long-term impact of the training program or a specific individual's or organization's increased capacity. And yet the proactive Training Department has used this experience as a springboard for several initiatives that are only now coming to fruition. The Museums Association recently partnered with the V&A in opening up the annual conference to the BAME heritage/cultural sector. The Capacity Building and Training Officer has interviewed key leaders in the sector on the business case for diversity, the recordings of which have been integrated into a training DVD. The GLA has commissioned the V&A to run training in equitable partnerships and the museum is partnering with Learning Skills Council and Kensington and Chelsea College to open up the V&A's NVQ training in heritage skills to BAME sector/individuals. Following the customized training for *Elevate*, the V&A is now planning heritage training for volunteers of the Anglo Sikh Heritage Trail. They, in return, have offered training to V&A staff on understanding the cultural background of the Sikh community.

The final words of the evaluator outline the direction the Museum should take:

> Cultural change in the museum and developing partnerships are the two weaker outcomes of the project compared with the research and event activities. However, these aspects were also the more challenging and ambitious. A whole-museum, centrally driven, networked-system approach, generating new knowledge, may deliver the next stage of development for the museum, building on a successful platform of achievement.
>
> What is remarkable is how much has been achieved in three years in such a complex project with so many outputs, working in a sophisticated international institution with other priorities demanding management time. It does suggest serious consideration should be given to integrating diversity into policy priorities.[28]

We may have reversed over a hundred years of history through the change of policy and practice with regard to the African collections, but other changes may take a little longer. What is self-evident is that we are on a journey where diversity becomes central to all that we do. To this end, we are working toward a more systematic approach, where diversity and equality are considered in the initial planning of any strategy, policy, gallery development, exhibition, etc., and monitored accordingly. With the coming of a new Single Equality Bill, we are aware of the need to move forward on other areas of equality while sustaining and developing our work on cultural diversity. Clearly, people have many different identities, and the diversity strands overlap. Given that, however, socio-economic status has been identified as a key future priority for the Museum.

Notes

1. The opinions expressed in this article are those of the author and do not necessarily represent any particular institutional viewpoint or policy.
2. Original bid to HLF for the Capacity Building and Cultural Ownership Project—working with culturally diverse communities prepared by Eithne Nightingale 2003/4.
3. Capacity Building and Cultural Ownership Evaluation, Section 1: Technical, Project evaluation brief, Juliette Fritsch, Learning and Interpretation, 30 September 2005
4. Transcripts from interviews, V&A Capacity Building and Cultural Ownership Evaluation Report. Prepared by Professor Simon Roodhouse on behalf of Safe Hands Management Ltd, February 2009.
5. Transcripts from interviews, V&A Capacity Building and Cultural Ownership Evaluation Report. Prepared by Professor Simon Roodhouse on behalf of Safe Hands Management Ltd, February 2009.
6. (Appendix 1.0, Acquisition and Disposal Policy. Extract from the V&A Collections Management Policy 2003 quoted in the V&A Collecting Plan 2005,58). "The V&A does not collect African art, and most of the African material once held by the Museum has long since been transferred, largely to the British Museum." (A Grand Design, the Victoria and Albert Museum, London:V&A Publications, 1997, 257).
7. Locating Africa at the V&A: Reflecting on the Outcomes of the African Diaspora Research Project: Helen Mears, African Diaspora Research Fellow, May 2008 published in the V&A Capacity Building and Cultural Ownership Evaluation Report. Prepared by Professor Simon Roodhouse on behalf of Safe Hands Management Ltd, February 2009.
8. For outputs from Helen's research see: www.vam.ac.uk/collections/periods_styles/hidden-histories/index.html
9. The V&A's Collecting Plan 2005 notes that the Photography section, in particular, seeks to 'extend coverage of work from Latin America, Africa, Eastern Europe and Asia and countries unrepresented in the collection.'
10. V&A's Access, Inclusion and Diversity Strategy approved by V&A Trustees 17th April 2003.
11. Transcript from interviews, V&A Capacity Building and Cultural Ownership Evaluation Report. Prepared by Professor Simon Roodhouse on behalf of Safe Hands Management Ltd, February 2009.
12. Transcript from interviews, V&A Capacity Building and Cultural Ownership Evaluation Report. Prepared by Professor Simon Roodhouse on behalf of Safe Hands Management Ltd, February 2009.
13. Discussion between African Caribbean Audience Development Officer and Head of Diversity Strategy Unit.

14. Traces of the Trade. Gallery trails marking the Bicentenary of the Abolition of the British SlaveTrade. February 2007. www.vam.ac.uk/collections/contemporary/past_exhns/uncomfortabletruths/trails/index.html

15. Telephone interviews, V&A Capacity Building and Cultural Ownership Evaluation Report. Prepared by Professor Simon Roodhouse on behalf of Safe Hands Management Ltd, February 2009.

16. Telephone interviews, V&A Capacity Building and Cultural Ownership Evaluation Report. Prepared by Professor Simon Roodhouse on behalf of Safe Hands Management Ltd, February 2009.

17. Telephone interviews, V&A Capacity Building and Cultural Ownership Evaluation Report. Prepared by Professor Simon Roodhouse on behalf of Safe Hands Management Ltd, February 2009

18. Telephone interviews, V&A Capacity Building and Cultural Ownership Evaluation Report. Prepared by Professor Simon Roodhouse on behalf of Safe Hands Management Ltd, February 2009.

19. Telephone interviews, V&A Capacity Building and Cultural Ownership Evaluation Report. Prepared by Professor Simon Roodhouse on behalf of Safe Hands Management Ltd, February 2009.

20. http://www.vam.ac.uk/activ_events/community/intercultural/index.html

21. www.vam.ac.uk/collections/periods_styles/features/festivalOfLight/index.html; www.flickr.com/groups/celebrations_of_light/

22. Ideopolis International, authored, Cultural Capacity Building at the V&A: An Evaluation: Draft Interim Report, p.67, 2007.

23. V&A Capacity Building and Cultural Ownership Evaluation Report. Prepared by Professor Simon Roodhouse on behalf of Safe Hands Management Ltd, February 2009.

24. V&A Capacity Building and Cultural Ownership Evaluation Report. Prepared by Professor Simon Roodhouse on behalf of Safe Hands Management Ltd, February 2009.

25. www.vam.ac.uk/moc/childrens_lives/east_end_lives/index.html; www.vam.ac.uk /childrens_lives/holidays_entertainment/the_singing_playground/index.html; www.vam.ac.uk/moc/childrens_lives/east_end_lives/flickrgroup/index.html; www.vam .ac.uk/moc/learning/community_programme_past_projects_east_end/index.html.

26. www.vam.ac.uk/collections/theater_performance/features/record_today_tomorrow /index.html

27. V&A Capacity Building and Cultural Ownership Evaluation Report. Prepared by Professor Simon Roodhouse on behalf of Safe Hands Management Ltd, February 2009.

28. V&A Capacity Building and Cultural Ownership Evaluation Report. Prepared by Professor Simon Roodhouse on behalf of Safe Hands Management Ltd, February 2009.

Reprinted and updated from Inspiring Action: Museums and Social Change, available from www.museumsetc.com.

Eithne Nightingale is Head of Diversity Strategy at the V&A Museum of art and design in London where she takes a lead on developing and implementing a Museum wide access, inclusion and diversity strategy and as it affects all areas and activities of the Museum. She oversaw the 1 million pound HLF funded Cultural Ownership and Capacity Building Programme — working with diverse communities which encompassed research into collections, public programming and the development of partnerships with black and ethnic minority organisations. She has also managed a range of programmes and initiatives which have attracted diverse audiences for example refugees and asylum seekers, young people at risk and the homeless.

Eithne has worked in race relations, community development, regeneration and post 16 education in inner London for over 30 years. She has worked as a consultant on the development of Community Colleges in South Africa and before coming to the V&A, she ran the community and adult education service and regeneration programmes in the London Borough of Hackney, one of the most diverse and socio-economically deprived areas in the UK. She is also a photographer and a travel/fiction writer.

Beginning with Change
Resources for Building Diversity in Museums

Tara Turner

The articles included in this special issue of the *Journal of Museum Education* have illustrated the complexity of the term diversity, as well as the variety of ways museums can and have approached a recognition of and engagement with diverse audiences, communities, collections, staff, board and volunteers. As these case studies, in their mix of theory, practice, research and critical reflection illustrate, a commitment to acknowledging and developing diversity means a willingness to experiment with innovative practices, to build institutional support and to be accountable to the range of individuals and groups who make up your museum's public and the public at large. In addition to these outstanding examples, there are a number of policies, programs, and practices available upon which to model and further develop this process of deep change in your own museum. The selection of resources that follows offers a mix of frameworks for diversity planning, examples of best practices and innovative programming, as well as research, reports and theoretical essays intended to inspire and guide institutional and individual action in museums that will create more reflective, relevant and accessible public institutions.

GENERAL DIVERSITY RESOURCES

International Council of Museums (ICOM)
"Museums and Cultural Diversity: Policy Statement"
http://icom.museum/diversity.html
This document, written by the ICOM Working Group on Cross-Cultural Issues, offers a recommended action plan for addressing cross-cultural issues within the organization. It includes a history of ICOM's work in this area that provides a broad view of the shifting ways museums have responded to their diverse communities.

Journal of Museum Education, Volume 34, Number 3, Fall 2009, pp. 271–280.

Canadian Museums Association (CMA)
"Cultural Diversity Publications"
http://25538.vws.magma.ca/en/info_resources/reports_guidelines/
The CMA's website includes a number of diversity publications, for
example: "Models for Working with Cultural Communities," by David Goa,
"Community Mapping and Museums," by Sandra Massey and "The Search
for Knowledge: Research as Invitation and Response," by Henriette Kelker.

American Association of Museums (AMA)
"Diversity and Museums"
http://www.aam-us.org/museumresources/div/index.cfm
This site provides a number of documents, resources and opportunities
related to the AMA's strategic commitment to addressing issues of diversity
in the museum community.

Museums Australia
"Museums Australia Incorporated Cultural Diversity Policy"
http://www.museumsaustralia.org.au/dbdoc/culturaldiv.pdf
This document defines the rights of multiculturalism and lists collection
development, public programs, accessibility, human resources and gov-
ernance as places where museums can uphold these rights.

University of Leicester (UK)
"Leicester Research Archive"
https://lra.le.ac.uk/
This database provides access to the work of the Research Centre for
Museums and Galleries at the University of Leicester. Reports include: "In
the past we would just be invisible": research into the attitudes of disabled
people to museums and heritage", "Buried in the footnotes: the representation of disabled people in museum and gallery collections", "A catalyst for
change: the social impact of the Open Museum" and "Museums and social
inclusion: the GLLAM Report".

National Army Museum (NAM), UK
"Corporate Information"
http://www.national-army-museum.ac.uk/aboutUs/
The NAM's website offers policy documents outlining their disability, race,
and gender equity schemes as well as their "Strategy for Equity and Diversity, Access and Inclusion" and Annual Equality Reports.

INCLUSION AND DIVERSITY IN
MUSEUM COLLECTIONS AND PROGRAMMING

The Open University, Abasuba Community Peace Museum, Embu Community Peace Museum, Lari Memorial Peace Museum, National Museums of Kenya (NMK), Porini Association, SIMOO(Simba Maasai Outreach Organization), UK and Kenya
"Heritage, Museums and Memorialization in Kenya: Exploring the Past in the Present"
http://www.open.ac.uk/Arts/ferguson-centre/memorialisation/index.html
A website devoted to a three-year collaborative project: "Managing Heritage, Building Peace: Museums, memorialization and the uses of memory in Kenya". This project focuses on fostering heritage that is inclusive of ordinary Kenyans, local history and the variety of ethnic communities that make up the nation.

Museum Victoria, AU
"Cultural Diversity Collection"
http://museumvictoria.com.au/collections-research/our-collections /collections/cultural-diversity/
A description of Museum Victoria's "Cultural Diversity Collection," which focuses particularly on gay and lesbian material, youth culture, ageing, homelessness, cultural affirmation and discrimination, sociology and social work, and volunteerism.

Museum of New Zealand, Te Papa Tongarewa
"Work with Iwi and Museums"
http://tepapa.govt.nz/AboutUs/Pages/Workwithiwiandmuseums.aspx#
These web pages document the role of the Te Papa division that works with museums, iwi (tribal groups), and related New Zealand organizations, as well as the Iwi Exhibition Programme and the Karanga Aotearoa Repatriation Programme, which is responsible for returning ancestral remains to their communities of origin.

Minneapolis Institute of Arts, USA
"A New Audience for a New Century"
http://www.artsmia.org/new_audience.pdf
A report by the Minneapolis Institute of Arts on their efforts to diversify their audience. Their research methodology is documented in detail as are their focus group sessions and the marketing strategies that developed from these.

The Lower East Side Tenement Museum, New York, USA
"The Tenement Windows Exhibit"
http://www.tenement.org/tenement-windows.html
The Tenement Windows Exhibit brings together contemporary artists and
ESOL classes to create site-specific installations that illuminate connections between the students' experiences and the experiences of the im-
migrants represented in the museum.

The Imperial War Museum, UK
"Rethinking Disability: Conflict and Disability Sessions"
http://london.iwm.org.uk/server.php?show=nav.1011
A description of the museum's one-day workshop for students that
"focuses on human rights, the power of protest and anti-discriminatory legislation using disabled people's rights as a case study." Students inspect the
public spaces of the Museum to assess its accessibility and explore the
history of disability legislation with a visit to Parliament.

DISABILITY AND ACCESSIBILITY IN MUSEUMS

Museums, Libraries and Archives Council (MLA), UK
"Disability Directory for Museums and Galleries"
http://www.mla.gov.uk/resources/assets//D/disdir_pdf_6877.pdf
This directory is intended as a guide for all museums and galleries to
improve their services to disabled people.The report focuses on accommodating visitors with physical, sensory, speech, mental and language impairments, and learning disabilities.

Museums, Libraries and Archives Council (MLA), UK
"The Disability Portfolio"
http://www.mla.gov.uk/what/support/toolkits/libraries_disability/find_
out_about_disability
A collection of twelve guides outlining how to meet the needs of disabled
people as users and staff in museums, archives and libraries. Topics include
training, technology, budgetary issues, environments, outreach and employment.

*National Gallery of Canada and the Canadian Museum
of Contemporary Photography*
"Art for All: Inclusive, Accessible and Adapted Programs at the National
Gallery of Canada and the Canadian Museum of Contemporary Photography"
http://www.gallery.ca/files/ed_Art_for_All.pdf
This document describes the museum's accessible programming for
families and children, teens, adults, schools and lists other valuable resources.

Association of Science-Technology Centers (ASTC), USA
"Accessible Practices"
http://www.astc.org/resource/access/funding.htm
The ASTC website brings together a number of resources including information about legal obligations and the disability rights movement, tem-
plates for access surveys and plans, and a collection of best practices and
funding resources.

Art Education for the Blind, USA
"Art Beyond Sight"
http://www.artbeyondsight.org/
As a "one-stop resource for bringing art and culture to people with visual
impairments", this website offers web-based courses, education resources,
training handbooks and discussion groups.

Tate, UK
Tate Learning, "I-Map"
http://www.tate.org.uk/imap
An on-line art resource designed for visually impaired people. It employs
text, audio, image enhancement and deconstruction, animation and raised
images.

Museum of Modern Art (MoMA), USA
"Access Programs"
http://www.moma.org/learn/programs/access
A list of MoMA's educational programs and services that cater to individuals and groups with visual or hearing impairments, developmental or
learning disabilities, limited mobility, Alzheimer's, or those who are
homebound.

LESBIAN, GAY, BISEXUAL, TRANSGENDER, AND QUEER (LGBTQ) IN MUSEUMS

Gay and Lesbian Alliance of Museums Australia (GLAMA)
"Gay and Lesbian Policy Guidelines for Museum Programs and Practice"
http://www.museumsaustralia.org.au/site/page68.php
http://www.museumsaustralia.org.au/dbdoc/culturaldiv.pdf
GLAMA is a special interest group devoted to advocating for the needs and interests of the range of individuals and groups who identify as LGTBQ. The group has developed a policy document: "Gay and Lesbian Policy Guidelines for Museum Programs and Practice" that promotes the inclusion of gay and lesbian communities and includes specific recommendations for museum staff, for structuring of museum relations, for project management necessities, and tips for staff training.

Museums Australia National Conference, May 7-14, 2006
Kate Davison, "Queering Voices in Museums"
http://www.museumsaustralia.org.au/dbdoc/Conf%2006%20Davison%20 Concurrent.pdf
An essay from the former Assistant Curator of Lesbian and Gay Material, Culture Survey Project at Museum Victoria, Australia, which describes various aspects of that project including community engagement, exhibitions, partnerships and research.
Victoria and Albert Museum, UK
"LGBTQ Histories at the V&A"
http://www.vam.ac.uk/activ_events/courses/lectures_talks_tours/lgbtq /index.html
A description of the V&A's ongoing events, talks and programs that seek to uncover the lesbian, gay, bisexual, transgender and queer experiences and narratives from the V&A collections.

GLBT Historical Society, USA
http://www.glbthistory.org/
An archive and museum dedicated to collecting, preserving and interpreting the history of GLBT people and the communities that support them. The website includes excellent programming examples and resources on collecting LGBTQ artifacts and objects.

ALL AGES IN MUSEUMS

National Museum of Australia
"Energised, Engaged, Everywhere: Older Australians and Museums"
http://www.amonline.net.au/amarc/pdf/research/fullreport.pdf
This 2002 document reports on the needs and expectations of older visitors
and lists a number of strategies that museums can develop to attract and
satisfy these individuals.

Association of Science-Technology Centers (ASTC), USA
"Older Adults in Science Centers"
http://www.astc.org/resource/older/index.htm
This webpage offers a report on "The Longevity Revolution" and resources
on developing education programs and employment in museums for older
adults.

California Association of Museums (CAM) Conference, February 27, 2009
Lisa Folsom, Adam Mikos, and Joe Holt, "Ageing and Ageism in Museums"
Christy Sakamoka, "The Seniority Rules"
http://www.calmuseums.org/conferences_and_workshops/2009Session8B
.pdf; http://www.calmuseums.org/e-news/Sakamoto_seniors_public.pdf
A panel discussion moderated by Nancy Arms Simon of the barriers facing
the aging population in museums and an essay by Christy Sakamoka, CAM
Fellow, that elaborates on that discussion.
Museum of Modern Art (MoMA), USA
"The Red Studio"
http://redstudio.moma.org/
A program developed between high school students and MoMA staff, the
Red Studio explores teen's questions about art, artists and the role of the
museum.

Association of Children's Museums (ACM), USA
"Diversity in Action"
http://www.childrensmuseums.org/programs/diversity.htm
On this website, the ACM's Diversity Committee offers a diversity pledge
template and diversity statement, examples of successful programs, scholarship opportunities and other resources to assist museums in advancing
the goal of inclusiveness and diversity.

WEB ACCESSIBILITY

Web Accessibility Initiative (WAI)
http://www.w3.org/WAI/
This website offers a multitude of strategies, guidelines and resources to make the web accessible to all people with disabilities.

WebAIM
"Web Accessibility in Mind"
http://www.webaim.org
A web resource with information about and guides to accessibility training, evaluation, design and delivery and a variety of web accessibility resources.

Stephen Brown and David Gerrard, *"Squaring the Triangle: The Implications of Broadband for Access, Diversity and Accessibility in Museum Web Design"*
Museums and the Web Conference, March 22-25, 2006
http://www.archimuse.com/mw2006/papers/brown/brown.html
This essay explores the tension between attracting broad audiences through web design and making websites accessible for users with disabilities. Brown and Gerrard argue that websites should be designed with overall usability in mind and offer case studies to support their claims.

Jim Thatcher, Michael R. Burks, Christian Heilmann, Andrew Kirkpatrick, Patrick H. Lauke, Bruce Lawson, Shawn Lawton Henry, Bob Regan, Richard Rutter, Mark Urban, Cynthia Waddell. *Web Accessibility: Web Standards and Regulatory Compliance.* New York: Apress, 2006.
A comprehensive book that deals with the meaning of accessibility in law and policy, its impact on new technologies and strategies for implementing accessible websites.

Museum 3.0
A Network for Museums and Web 3.0
http://museum30.ning.com/
A network for those interested in technology and the future of museums, galleries, science centres and other collecting bodies.

DIVERSITY IN STAFF, BOARD AND VOLUNTEERS

Museums Australia
"Museums Australia Women's Policy Guidelines
for Museums Programs and Practice"
http://www.museumsaustralia.org.au/dbdoc/women.pdf
This document outlines gender discrimination in museums and offers
strategies to address these imbalances in areas of representation and employment.

Association of Science-Technology Centers (ASTC), USA
"ASTC Diversity and Leadership Development Fellows Program"
http://www.astc.org/resource/equity/fellows.htm
This is a program designed to support the professional development and
retention of professionals of color currently working in the museum field.

*Canadian Museums Association (CMA), Cultural Diversity
and Museums Publications*
Sandra Massey, "Community Mapping and Museums"
http://25538.vws.magma.ca/fr/info_et_ressources/rapports_et_lignes_di-
rectrices/community_mapping/index.php
A description of a CMA project undertaken by four Alberta museums
which created inventories of community resources with the goal of
achieving employment equity and organizational development within
museums.
International Committee for the Training of Personnel (ICTOP) Conference, Bar-
celona, July 2, 2001
Dr. Lynne Teather, "Transforming Museum Studies: Educating Museol-
ogists for Cultural Diversity"
http://www.utoronto.ca/mouseia/icom/TransformingMuseumStudies.html
An essay reflecting upon courses developed at the University of Toronto
Museum Studies programme dealing with cultural pluralism and
museums. This paper is an excellent resource for further reading on these
issues.

Imperial War Museum, UK
"Equality Strategy"
http://www.iwm.org.uk/server/show/ConWebDoc.4399
This webpage offers several policy documents that support the Imperial
War Museum's concerted efforts to improve workforce diversity.

Institute of International Visual Arts
Culturally Diverse Arts Professional Network
http://www.iniva.org/learning/professional_development/arts
_professional_network
A monthly meeting and networking opportunity for culturally diverse arts
professionals intended to provide an opportunity for discussion, information sharing and networking.

*Tara Turner is a graduate of the Museum Studies programme at the University of
Toronto where her research focused on post-conflict heritage. She is an Education
Officer and Program Assistant in the Education Department at the Art Gallery of
Ontario.*

The topic of achieving increased diversity in museums is certainly not new. One can easily see its progression from the recommendations offered in the 1984 publication, *Museums for a New Century*[1], to the goals, standards and strategies defined in the 1992 publication, *Excellence and Equity*[2], to the most recent research and workshops centered on understanding population trends in the United States and its implications for museums as conducted by the Center for the Future of Museums.[3] Museum leaders have carved a path which, if followed, could lead to achieving a new, more diverse, more relevant and more accessible future for museums and the public. Clearly, the profession has its marching orders. So why is this work so difficult? Why is it that, according to researchers at the Center for the Future of Museums, only one in ten core museum visitors today is non-Anglo, and only 20% of museum workers are non-Anglo?[4]

In this issue of the *Journal of Museum Education* Gillian McIntyre and Syrus Marcus Ware argue that we have not fully achieved a more pluralistic museum in part because diversity in museums has not yet been thoroughly reflected in the practice of our work. Moreover, they state that the language around diversity is still not coherent across museums.

I would like to add the notion that achieving pluralistic museums is not gained solely by following an established vision, aligning programs and exhibits around sets of goals and standards, and looking at demographic trends. While all of these elements are vital in achieving a new public dimension for museums, what we don't have in place is a way of assessing how we are doing both individually and organizationally as we strive to achieve cultural proficiency. Demographic information gathering is one measure of our progress, but such data do not show how the organization or the individuals who work in the organization have adjusted their systems and approaches to both respond to difference and to reach different audiences.

Museum staff need an approach to engage in discussion about all types of diversity that is not judgmental, but is instead a coming together of personal and organizational identity. Further, given the complexity of the issue and of our work in museums, I believe it prudent NOT to assign a scale as our rubric, but rather a continuum upon which to assess our progress. Such a continuum might have distinct points along the way, but both individually and organizationally one could find themselves on different points along it at different moments in time. It is not a continuum in which we ever

Journal of Museum Education, Volume 34, Number 3, Fall 2009, pp. 281–285.

"arrive," but is instead a framework which enables us to always ask the question 'how am I doing?' and 'how is my museum doing?'

The framework I am suggesting is a cultural proficiency continuum developed in 1989 by Terry Cross, executive director of the National Indian Child Welfare Association in Portland, Oregon[5]. Used in schools, businesses, government agencies and not-for-profits, the cultural proficiency continuum addresses diversity on both an individual and organizational/systems level. Randall Lindsey, Kikanza Nuri Robins and Raymond Terrell applied Cross' continuum for use by leaders in school settings. They describe the continuum as, 'an approach for responding to the environment shaped by its diversity. It is not an off-the-shelf program that supplements a school's programs. It is a model for shifting the culture of the school or district – a model for individual transformation and organizational change.'[6] Note the importance of the words 'the environment shaped by its diversity.' Lindsey, Robins and Terrell stress that the diversity of the school population is already shaping the school culture, and that the appropriate response to the shift in the minority-majority population requires environmental adaptation in schools, not the retro-fitting of old systems. Meanwhile, it seems that museums address the issue of diversity from the perspective of drawing-in a wider array of diverse visitors. What if museums focused instead on shaping the museum environment by the diversity it currently holds? What if the focus was to deepen and broaden the experience for the diverse audiences already coming through the doors? Will such organizational change ultimately lead to increased numbers of diverse visitors? According to the National Center for Cultural Competence at Georgetown University, "Cross et al. state that cultural competence is a complex framework, and that there is a tendency for systems and organizations to want a textbook solution, a quick fix, a recipe, or a "how to", step-by-step approach. The complexity of achieving cultural competence does not allow for such an easy solution."[7]

What follows is Cross' framework, called the Cultural Proficiency Continuum. I have also provided some starting points for opening the dialogue in your institution, should you chose to apply this continuum in your setting:

THE CULTURAL PROFICIENCY CONTINUUM

There are six points along the continuum that describe unique ways of *seeing* and *responding* to difference:

Cultural destructiveness – *see the difference, stomp it out*: the elimination of other people's cultures

Cultural incapacity – *see the difference, make it wrong*: Belief in the superiority of one's culture and behavior that disempowers another's culture

Cultural blindness – *see the difference, act like you don't*: Acting as if the cultural differences you see do not matter, or not recognizing that there are differences among and between cultures

Cultural pre-competence – *see the difference, respond inadequately*: Awareness of the limitations of one's skills or an organization's practices when interacting with other cultural groups

Cultural competence – *see the difference, understand the difference that difference makes*: Interacting with other cultural groups using the five essential elements of cultural proficiency as the standard for individual behavior and organizational practices
> Name the differences: Assess culture
> Claim the differences: Value diversity
> Reframe the differences: Manage the dynamics of difference
> Train about differences: Adapt to diversity
> Change for differences: Institutionalize cultural knowledge

Cultural proficiency – *see the difference and respond positively and affirmingly*: *Esteeming culture, knowing how to learn about individual and organizational culture, and interacting effectively in a variety of cultural environments*[8]

How can you use this framework in your museum? Begin an honest dialogue with yourself and your colleagues about how you see and respond to difference. Be open to the idea that you as an individual may be in a different place along the continuum than your colleagues or your organization. And then be willing to extend the conversation, seeking ways in which both you and your colleagues can move further along the continuum toward cultural proficiency.

Use the continuum to assess how your organization is doing. Pose a set of questions for groups to consider when looking at the systems in your museum. For whom and by whom are those sytems set up? Here are some examples of systems questions to get you started: How are your exhibitions curated, and how many perspectives are considered and involved in the creation of exhibits? How is the curriculum for educational programs developed? In what languages is way finding signage written? For whom are the audio-tours created, and do they meet the needs of a diverse public? What non-English language books and other items are available in the gift shop? With whom is your institution partnering, and what is the nature of such partnerships? How are museum volunteers recruited? How is staff recruited and hired?

Look for other tools to use when engaging in conversations about diversity. For example, download and use the discussion guide associated with this JME (available on the Museum Education Roundtable website (http://www.museumeducation.info). Look at the resources outlined in Tara Turner's article in this issue of the JME, Beginning with Change: Resources for Building Diversity in Museums , and view the most recent webcast by Gregory Rodriguez offered by the Center for the Future of Museums (http://www.futureofmuseums.org/).

I am hopeful that this continuum will open up doors to conversation and enable change within your institution. Use this continuum as a framework for dialogue, and couple it with the goals, strategies and vision of the future of museums.

Tina R. Nolan *(Tina.Nolan@nl.edu) is currently Chair of the Publications Committee of the Museum Education Roundtable and is serving as interim Editor-in-Chief of the Journal of Museum Education. Ms. Nolan has spent the past 18 years working in cultural institutions ranging in type from zoos to nature centers to museums. In February 1999, Ms. Nolan helped to open the new public institution of the Chicago Academy of Sciences, the Peggy Notebaert Nature Museum. In 2001, Ms. Nolan became Director of Education at the Nature Museum. Ms. Nolan joined National-Louis University in 2006 as Associate Director of Partnerships in the National College of Education. In this capacity, Ms. Nolan establishes new partnerships between NLU's National College of Education and school districts, education reform organizations, cultural institutions and community organizations nationally and internationally. Ms. Nolan continues to work with museums and other not-for-profit educational organizations as an independent education consultant.*

Ms. Nolan has a Masters degree in Education at National-Louis University and is currently a doctoral candidate where the focus of her research is centered on educational leadership in cultural institutions.

Notes

1. Joel N. Bloom and Earl A. Powell III, *Museums for a New Century: A Report of the Commission on Museums for a New Century* (Washington, D.C.: American Association of Museums, 1984).
2. American Association of Museums, *Excellence and Equity: Education and the Public Dimension of Museums* (Washington, D.C.: 1992).
3. American Association of Museums and Museums for a New Century, *Museums and Society 2034: Trends and Potential Futures* (Washington, D.C. 2008).
4. Ibid.
5. Cross, T., Bazron, B., Dennis, K., & Isaacs, M. (1989). *Towards a Culturally Competent System of Care, Volume 1.* Washington, DC: CASSP Technical Assistance Center, Center for Child Health and Mental Health Policy, Georgetown University Child Development Center
6. Randall B. Lindsey, Kikanza Nuri Robins & Raymond D. Terrell, *Cultural Proficiency: A Manual for School Leaders* (Thousand Oaks, CA: Corwin Press, 2003), 5-6.
7. National Center for Cultural Competence, Georgetown University Center for Child and Human Development, *Cultural Competence Continuum*, Tawara D. Goode, compiler (Washington, D.C.: Georgetown University, 2004).
8. Cross, T., Bazron, B., Dennis, K., & Isaacs, M. (1989). *Towards a Culturally Competent System of Care, Volume 1.* Washington, DC: CASSP Technical Assistance Center, Center for Child Health and Mental Health Policy, Georgetown University Child Development Center

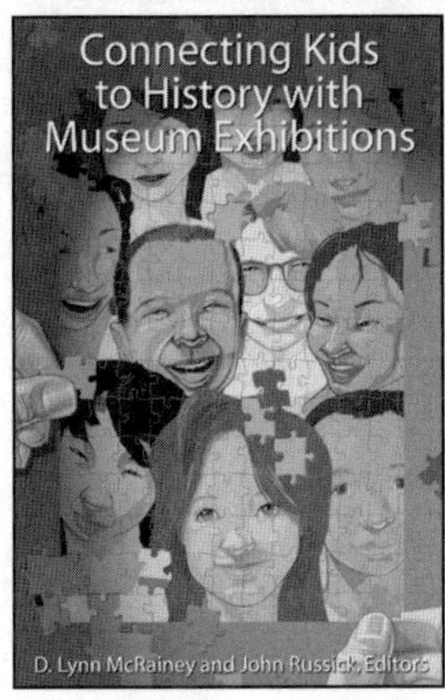

CONNECTING KIDS TO HISTORY WITH MUSEUM EXHIBITIONS

D. Lynn McRainey and John Russick, Editors

Kids have profound and important relationships to the past, but they don't experience history in the same way as adults. D. Lynn McRainey and John Russick have brought together top museum professionals who present current research and practice to make Connecting Kids to History With Museum Exhibitions the essential new guide to creating meaningful and memorable museum experiences for children.

"What a wonderful addition to our professional literautre. Grounded in current research, stuffed with telling examples, organized around the logic of how exhibits are actually imagined and brought to life, this collection of essays will be useful to all of us trying to understand the theory and processes of creating experiences that appeal to and absorb kids, or for families looking for ways to share in each other's enthusiasms, or in support of teachers looking for insights to bring back to and chew on in their classrooms. There are productive things to mine, not just for history museums and historic sites, but for art, science and children's museums."

—**Michael Spock**, Chapin Hall Center for Children, University of Chicago

"I can't wait to have this book in the hands of my students! This amazing group of authors presents the most current research and innovative thinking. The breadth of examples and frameworks solidly place kids as a core and not peripheral museum audience. The authors speak to each other and build on each other's work, creating a wonderful conversation with a coherent message. They don't just advocate, they provide concrete guidance, models and powerful examples drawn from theory, research and practice. This book goes beyond the audience of kids and the discipline of history, and is extremely valuable for exhibit designers, educators, evaluators, curators, administrators and any museum professional interested in how to make the museum more engaging for kids."

—**Kris Morrissey**, Director, Museology Graduate Program, University of Washington

FEBRUARY 2010, 334 PAGES, OVER 40 PHOTOGRAPHS
HARDBACK ISBN 978-1-59874-382-1, $89.00 / **WEB PRICE $75.65**
PAPERBACK ISBN 978-1-59874-383-8, $34.95 / **WEB PRICE $29.71**

15% OFF WEB ORDERS! *All books, all the time.*

TO ORDER 800-621-2736 ❖ *www.LCoastPress.com* ❖ *Explore@LCoastPress.com*